Corolyn Faville Ober, Cynthia M. Westover

Manhattan, Historic and Artistic

A six Day Tour of New York City

Corolyn Faville Ober, Cynthia M. Westover

Manhattan, Historic and Artistic
A six Day Tour of New York City

ISBN/EAN: 9783337192853

Printed in Europe, USA, Canada, Australia, Japan

Cover: Foto ©Andreas Hilbeck / pixelio.de

More available books at **www.hansebooks.com**

MANHATTAN

HISTORIC AND ARTISTIC

A SIX DAY TOUR OF NEW YORK CITY

BY
COROLYN FAVILLE OBER
AND
CYNTHIA M. WESTOVER

NEW YORK
LOVELL, CORYELL & COMPANY
43, 45 AND 47 EAST TENTH STREET

COPYRIGHT, 1892,
BY
COROLYN FAVILLE OBER
AND
CYNTHIA M. WESTOVER

PREFACE

It has not been the intention of the authors of this book to compile a dictionary or a directory of the City of New York, but to provide, in as attractive a literary form as the nature of the work would permit, a guide-book that should economize time for the sightseer by its presentment, in orderly sequence, of the best that the city contains.

Although special attention has been paid to the historic and artistic features of the metropolis, its educational, commercial, municipal, philanthropic, and charitable institutions have each been represented, as has also its social life, and even its squalor, thus making a description of New York in its complex entirety.

The time-table and itinerary is permissive, not mandatory—to make use of a legal expression—and will serve to give an idea of the proportionate amount of time required to visit each object of interest, or to go from one place to another. It is absolutely reliable, every foot of the ground having been gone over and the time carefully registered. The variations to which such a table is likely to be subjected are so slight as to make no material difference, the length of the days in the summer or winter seasons, or the temporary closing of an art gallery, being about the only changes that are likely to occur. The hours when visitors are admitted to different institutions are always mentioned, and calculated for in the itinerary.

Sightseers will find their efforts greatly facilitated by reading the book before undertaking to follow any of the routes mapped out for them. Many places not indicated in the time-table, but described in the text, are too interesting to be passed by unobserved, and they may be of sufficient importance to some individuals to induce a change of plan. Plain directions accompanying each description will enable the stranger to avoid mistakes.

As the routes are plainly marked on the maps it will be seen that whoever takes this book as a guide will be safely chaperoned. It should therefore be considered a valuable aid to residents who are unable to devote their time to conducting guests about the city.

The work also aims to be a serviceable book of reference. As a Primer of the History of

New York it is a condensed compilation of the best authorities, and brings the past into a juxtaposition with the present that makes every locality vital and instructive with its report of progress.

To the courtesy which the authors invariably have received from historians, librarians, officials, and other persons to whom they have applied for information or special privileges, the possibility of inaugurating a successful career for this work is largely due. It is now the pleasant duty of the writers to acknowledge this indebtedness.

C. F. O.
C. M. W.

TIME-TABLE AND ITINERARY.

THE FIRST MORNING.

			DESCRIPTION PAGE
9.	A.M.	Battery Terminus.	1–7
9.25	"	Fraunce's Tavern.	7–8
9.50	"	Produce Exchange.	10–11
10.20	"	Trinity Church.	13–16
10.40	"	Stock Exchange.	17
10.50	"	Wall Street.	16–21
11.	"	Assay Office.	18
11.15	"	Treasury Building.	18–21
11.40	"	Equitable Building.	22
12.	M.	Luncheon at the Café Savarin in the Equitable Building.	

THE FIRST AFTERNOON.

1.15 P.M.		"The Russian Wedding Feast," a picture exhibited at No. 24 John Street	25–26
1.45	"	St. Paul's.	26–27
1.55	"	City Hall Park.	30–32
2.10	"	The Governor's Room.	31
2.35	"	Pulitzer Building.	33–34
3.05	"	Frankfort Street.	36
3.35	"	Brooklyn Bridge.	36
4.20	"	Broadway Cars.	39
4.45	"	Denning's, formerly A. T. Stewart's, Dry Goods Store.	40–41
5.15	"	Grace Church.	42

THE SECOND MORNING.

9.	A.M.	"After the Hunt," a picture exhibited at No. 8 Warren Street.	44
9.35	"	Park Row.	45
9.45	"	Chatham Square.	45–46

THE SECOND MORNING—Continued. DESCRIPTION PAGE

9.55	"	THE FIVE POINTS HOUSE OF INDUSTRY.	46–47
10.40	"	THE TOMBS.	47–49
11.35	"	MOTT STREET.	49–50
11.45	"	ELEVATED RAILWAY STATION AT CHATHAM SQUARE.	

THE SECOND AFTERNOON.

12.10	P.M.	THE ASTOR LIBRARY.	51–52
12.45	"	LUNCHEON AT VIENNA BAKERY, CORNER OF BROADWAY AND TENTH STREET.	
2.	"	COOPER UNION.	56–58
2.40	"	STUYVESANT SQUARE.	62–64
2.55	"	UNION SQUARE.	66–69
3.15	"	MACY'S.	69–71
3.45	"	YOUNG WOMEN'S CHRISTIAN ASSOCIATION.	72
4.15	"	TIFFANY'S.	72–75

THE THIRD MORNING.

9.	A.M.	ART ROOM OF J. H. JOHNSTON'S JEWELRY STORE.	76–78
9.35	"	"CHOOSING THE BRIDE," A PAINTING EXHIBITED AT SCHUMANN'S JEWELRY STORE.	78
10.15	"	GRAMERCY PARK.	78–79
10.30	"	ROOMS OF THE ASSOCIATED ARTISTS.	80–81
11.05	"	ACADEMY OF DESIGN.	81–83

THE THIRD AFTERNOON.

1.	P.M.	LUNCHEON AT DELMONICO'S, CORNER OF FIFTH AVENUE AND 26TH STREET.	
2.	"	AMERICAN ART GALLERIES.	84
3.15	"	MADISON SQUARE	84–86
3.30	"	COUPIL'S ART GALLERY.	89
4.	"	WORKS OF ART IN THE HOFFMAN HOUSE.	90–92
4.50	"	BROADWAY CARS, GOING NORTHWARD.	92–94

THE FOURTH MORNING.

DESCRIPTION
PAGE

9.	A.M.	FOURTH AVENUE CARS AT UNION SQUARE.	95–101
9.25	"	A TOUR IN 66TH STREET, TO THIRD AVENUE.	
			101–102
		THIRD AVENUE TO 67TH STREET.	102
		67TH STREET TO LEXINGTON AVENUE.	102–103
		LEXINGTON AVENUE TO 68TH STREET.	103
		68TH STREET TO FOURTH AVENUE.	103
		FOURTH AVENUE TO 72D STREET.	103–104
		72D STREET TO FIFTH AVENUE.	104
10.	"	LENOX LIBRARY.	104–107
11.	"	FIFTH AVENUE STAGE.	107–109
11.15	"	ST. PATRICK'S CATHEDRAL.	109–111
11.35	"	FIFTH AVENUE STAGE.	111–119
12.	M.	WASHINGTON SQUARE.	119–123

THE FOURTH AFTERNOON.

12.30 P.M. LUNCHEON AT THE ST. DENIS HOTEL, CORNER OF 11TH STREET AND BROADWAY.

THE DRIVE. . . 124–133

2. " "THE CIRCLE," CORNER OF 59TH STREET AND EIGHTH AVENUE.—BOULEVARD TO 110TH STREET.—110TH STREET TO MORNINGSIDE AVENUE-WEST.—MORNINGSIDE AVENUE WEST TO 122D STREET.—AMSTERDAM, OR TENTH AVENUE, TO 142D STREET.—142D STREET TO CONVENT AVENUE.—CONVENT AVENUE TO 143D STREET.—143D STREET TO THE BOULEVARD, OR ELEVENTH AVENUE.—BOULEVARD TO 161ST STREET.—ST. NICHOLAS AVENUE TO 181ST STREET.—181ST STREET TO WASHINGTON BRIDGE.—SEDGEWICK AVENUE TO MCCOMB'S DAM, OR CENTRAL BRIDGE.—SEVENTH AVENUE TO 145TH STREET.—45TH STREET TO BOULEVARD.—BOULEVARD

THE FOURTH AFTERNOON—Continued. DESCRIPTION PAGE

TO 131ST STREET.—131ST STREET TO TWELFTH AVENUE.—TWELFTH AVENUE TO RIVERSIDE PARK.—RIVERSIDE DRIVE.

THE FIFTH MORNING.

CENTRAL PARK.

9.	A.M.	THE ZOOLOGICAL GARDENS, CORNER OF 64TH STREET AND FIFTH AVENUE.	137
9.30	"	MALL AND TERRACE.	138–142
10.	"	PARK PHAETON AT TERRACE.	142–143
10.15	"	THE AMERICAN MUSEUM OF NATURAL HISTORY.	143–153
11.45	"	PARK PHAETON.	153–154
12.	M.	LUNCHEON IN CENTRAL PARK AT McGOWAN'S PASS TAVERN.	

THE FIFTH AFTERNOON.

1.	P.M.	POINTS OF HISTORICAL INTEREST. McGOWAN'S PASS, BLOCK HOUSE, ETC.	155–157
2.	"	PARK PHAETON.	157–158
2.15	"	THE METROPOLITAN MUSEUM OF ART.	158–172
5.	"	PARK PHAETON.	172

THE SIXTH MORNING.

THE ISLANDS.

9.	A.M.	BEDLOE'S, OR LIBERTY, ISLAND	174–177
10.30	"	ELLIS ISLAND.	177–179
11.30	"	GOVERNOR'S ISLAND.	179–181

THE SIXTH AFTERNOON.

12.30	P.M.	LUNCHEON AT DELMONICO'S, JUNCTION OF BEAVER AND WILLIAM STREETS.	
2.	"	BOAT FOR GLEN ISLAND LEAVES PIER AT THE FOOT OF CORTLANDT STREET FOR A SAIL ON THE EAST RIVER, PASSING BLACKWELL'S, WARD'S, AND RANDALL'S ISLANDS.	182–194

MANHATTAN.

CHAPTER I.

THE FIRST MORNING.—THE BATTERY.

DUTCH OCCUPATION.—Within the region of the little park which is situated at the southern extremity of the city are clustered many of the most interesting associations of the past. In 1626 Manhattan Island was purchased by the Dutch West India Company from the Indians for beads, buttons, and trinkets, equivalent in value to about twenty-four dollars. A blockhouse having been erected as a fortification, the settlers, who soon came from Holland, formed about it a little colony which they called New Amsterdam. The fortress, which was named Fort Amsterdam and inhabited by Dutch governors for over fifty years, stood on the spot now occupied by the steamship offices opposite Bowling Green,—the water edge being then nearer than at present.

As at this time Manhattan Island was within

the limits of the northern colony of Virginia,
it belonged in reality to the British crown, but
its possession was not disputed until the year
1664, when Charles the Second granted to his
brother, the Duke of York and Albany, territory now comprising the States of New York,
New Jersey, and Delaware. Immediately after
the transfer of this property the new owner

THE OLD FORT AT THE BATTERY.

dispatched troops who forced the Dutch governor (Stuyvesant) to surrender,—when the
name of the colony was changed to New York
in honor of the conqueror. From this time
Manhattan Island was alternately in the hands
of the Dutch and the English until 1691, when
Great Britain regained possession and remained
in power during the interval that preceded
the Revolution.

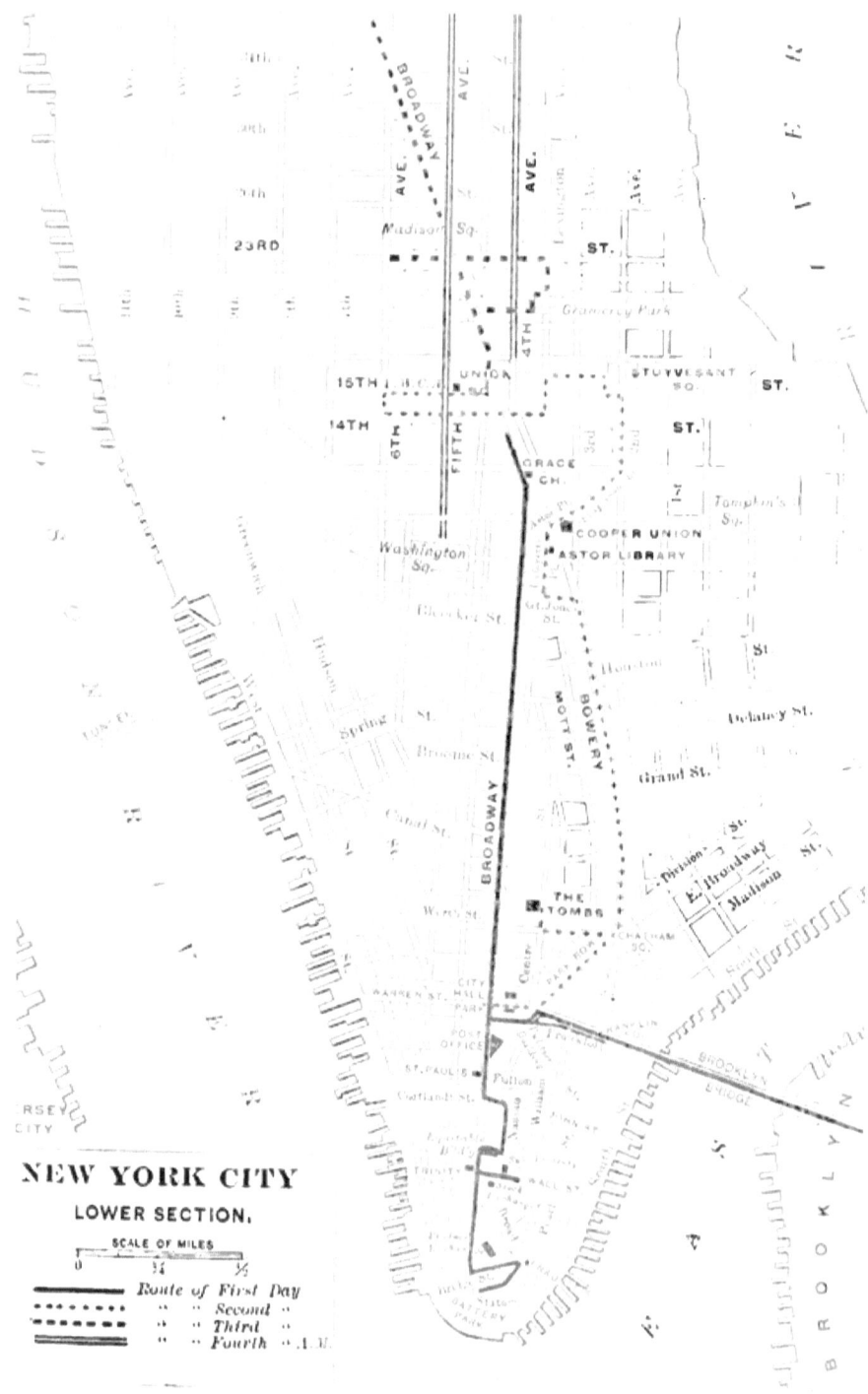

BRITISH OCCUPATION.—This peaceful epoch constituted the golden age of colonial history. As late as the year 1700, there were but three hundred houses on this portion of the Island, and on moonless nights the streets were lighted by lanterns, containing candles, hung on a pole from the window of every seventh house. The region of the Battery was the court end of the town, where the English governors and their suites, together with wealthy Dutch families, formed a circle famous for its culture, wit, and beauty. During this *régime* the etiquette of foreign courts was punctiliously observed.

AMERICAN OCCUPATION.—After the establishment of American independence the old fort was torn down, and a mansion, intended as a residence for the President, was built upon its site; but as this edifice was not completed until after the removal of the capital from New York, it was never occupied by the President, but became the gubernatorial residence until the retirement of John Jay. After this time the apartments were used as offices until the mansion was replaced by the six dwelling-houses that still remain.

In 1805, a new fort, erected at a little distance from the old site, was named Fort Clinton, but its shape gave it the popular soubriquet of "Castle." As originally built, the fort was separated from the mainland by a strip of water, bridged by a draw. It was a circular building of solid stone masonry, the walls of which were in some places thirty feet thick, mounted with barbette and casement guns, and regarded as a triumph of skill and solidity, although against modern guns it would have been a mere egg-shell. As the chief defence of the City of New York, it was liberally armed and garrisoned by the Government.

When in 1814, the blockade which the English had established at the southern ports became extended along the coast, the possibility of a naval attack caused the citizens of New York to erect works on Brooklyn Heights, on the islands in the bay, along the shores of the lower bay, and at different points on the Hudson and East Rivers; thus making Fort Clinton practically useless for military purposes. It was therefore not long before Government deeded the property to the State, since which time it has been called Castle Garden, and has been used for civic purposes only.

CASTLE GARDEN.—After the fort and the surrounding grounds became state property, the whole aspect of the place was changed. Groves of trees were planted, and the parks thus made became the favorite resort of the fashionable. Elegant mansions occupied the whole of State Street, some of which remain, shorn of balconies and piazzas and giving little evidence of their former grandeur. From the windows of these residences were witnessed the pageants occasioned by the inauguration of Washington, and the opening of the Erie Canal,—when De Witt Clinton, with great solemnity, poured the waters from Lake Erie into those of the bay. Whitehall Street also was lined with stately homes, but a great fire swept them all away. On festive occasions the trees in front of the drawbridge were lighted with colored lamps, and the draw was decorated with bunting, while bird-cages and hanging baskets were hung in the casements. Brilliant receptions were held within the fortress in honor of Lafayette, President Jackson, President Tyler, and Henry Clay. At the landing a funeral cortège met the remains of John Quincy Adams. In 1850 a great union meeting was here addressed by Henry Clay, General Cass, Daniel Webster, R. C. Winthrop, and Ogden Hoffman. Indeed, all mass meetings and celebrations assembled at this place until the uptown movement made New Yorkers require more central accommodations.

In 1847 Castle Garden was fitted up as a theatre and opera-house, and its stage was the scene of Jenny Lind's triumph three years later. The Julien Concerts and the voice of Madame Sontag made the year 1852 an equally memorable one in the annals of its musical history.

In 1855 a great change occurred in this historic building; it was then leased to the State Board of Emigration, and used as a landing-depot for immigrants. Government recently having taken to itself the duty of receiving this class of foreigners, has constructed more elaborate accommodations for them on Ellis Island, and the fate of Castle Garden is therefore at this time uncertain. It is now temporarily utilized by the Free Labor Bureau, —an institution maintained by the German and Irish Emigration Societies.

THE BATTERY AT THE PRESENT TIME.— Shipping and warehouses, business offices, etc. now surround the park on the land side, almost obliterating the historic landmarks. The termini of all elevated roads, and the Broadway and Belt Line surface cars, are at the southern extremity, where are also ferries to Brooklyn, Staten Island, Coney Island, Governor's Island, and Bedloe's Island. The granite structure near by, with a tower ninety feet in height, containing a flash light, is the United States Barge Office,—a building intended to accommodate the Surveyor of the Port. Floating bath-houses, that furnish free bathing facilities during the warm season, are moored to the Battery walls. A statue of Captain John Ericsson soon is to be placed in this park, where it will face the incoming steamers.

POINTS OF INTEREST BETWEEN THE BATTERY AND BOWLING GREEN.—The first Custom House, erected during the administration of Peter Stuyvesant, stood at the corner of State and Whitehall Streets. In Pearl Street, between State and Whitehall, stood the first church and parsonage of New Amsterdam, surrounded by the walls of the fort. South of this, in Whitehall Street, the United States Army Building rears an imposing front.

THE OLD FRAUNCE'S TAVERN still stands at the southeastern corner of Pearl and Broad Streets. This building, originally the home of Etienne De Lancey,—the father of the lieutenant-governor,—was converted into an inn after the owner had built a more palatial residence in Broadway. The "great room" of the establishment once was utilized as a Chamber of Commerce, and in it occurred the closing scene of the Revolution,—the parting of Washington with his officers, previous to the surrender of his commission to the Continental Congress. The supreme moment had arrived when these brothers-in-arms, whose mutual efforts and sufferings had achieved a sublime victory, must part from their leader and from each other. Filling a glass with wine, Washington said to his officers: "With a heart full of love and gratitude I now take leave of you, and most devoutly wish that your latter days may be as prosperous and happy as your former ones have been glorious and honorable. I cannot come to each of you to take my leave, but I shall be obliged if each one will come and take my hand." Each embraced him in turn, too much overcome with emotion for speech, after which the General silently withdrew from the room and entered a barge which awaited him at the foot of Whitehall Street. The room hallowed by this memorable event is still preserved. Relics of the past adorn its walls, and an old table is shown which is supposed to have been one of the original articles of furniture. The building has several times been repaired, but some of the Holland bricks are still visible in the walls, while others of them are collected in the cellar and are given to relic-hunters by the obliging proprietor.

During the latter half of the last century a Royal Exchange for Merchants stood at the foot of Broad Street. This curiously constructed building consisted of one large room supported by arches

In State Street, near the corner of Bridge Street, the home of Washington Irving, and the famous Knickerbocker inn of Peter Bayard, were situated.

BOWLING GREEN.—The encircled space at the foot of Broadway has been known as "Bowling Green" ever since the early days when it was a market-place in front of the fort, and a field for the sports of Dutch lads and lassies.

Here was the scene of the riot of 1765, when the "Sons of Liberty" opposed the Stamp Act, burning the effigy of the English governor, and casting his coach into a bonfire that had been made of a wooden fence which then surrounded the Green. When the cities of the colony afterward united to form a Stamp-Act Congress, and thus secured the repeal of this obnoxious law, the gratitude of the citizens induced them to erect a leaden equestrian statue of George the Third upon the centre of the Green. This was pulled down in 1776, at the time of the reading of the Declaration of Independence, and was afterward melted into bullets and used for the defence of American liberty. The iron balls with which the pickets of the fence surrounding the statue had been decorated were at the same time taken for cannon-shot.

Another event which marked the fame of this locality was the parade of 1788, on the occasion of the adoption of the Constitution by New York State. This was the first important pageant ever seen in America, and in it every class of the population appeared, even the most noted personages. The President and members of Congress, while watching the procession from the walls of the fort, were saluted with a salvo of thirteen guns from a float representing a Federal ship, emblazoned with the name of Alexander Hamilton, and manned by thirty sailors, with a full complement of officers.

In 1789 the face of the first President of the Republic appeared on a huge transparency which adorned the Green on the evening of his inauguration.

A fountain and flower-beds inclosed with an iron railing now occupy this historical site.

LOWER BROADWAY FROM BOWLING GREEN TO TRINITY CHURCH.—East of Bowling Green, the first object which attracts attention is the Produce Exchange, a magnificent structure of granite, terra-cotta, and red brick, and one of the finest specimens of architecture in New York, the style being a modification of Italian Renaissance. The gallery is open to visitors during the hours of exchange—from 10 A.M. until 3 P.M.—and the clock-tower, or campa-

nile, from which a beautiful view of the city
and bay may be obtained, is accessible, when
tickets are procured from the superintendent,
at all times, except Saturdays, in the afternoon,
and Sundays. From the corner of Beaver
Street may be seen a portion of the Cotton
Exchange,—a handsome edifice of yellow
brick with stone facings.

THE WASHINGTON BUILDING, at the corner
of Battery Place and Broadway, is a gigantic
structure twelve stories in height, which was
erected by Cyrus W. Field. The detail of its
architectural plan is crude French Renaissance.
This side of Broadway was once occupied by
the residences of wealthy and famous persons.

THE KENNEDY HOUSE, built in 1760 by
Archibald Kennedy, Collector of the Port,
stood at the corner. It was a spacious and elegant mansion situated in the midst of beautiful grounds that extended to the water's edge.
General Putnam made this house his headquarters previous to the battle of Long Island;
and it was also occupied at various times by
Lord Cornwallis, Lord Howe, Sir Henry Clinton, and Talleyrand. Here Benedict Arnold
arranged his conspiracy against his country;
and from here Washington witnessed the departure of the British troops. In its later
years this residence was converted into the

Washington Hotel. The second house was a spacious, old-time edifice, built and originally occupied by the Honorable John Watts. It is also said to have been the home of Benedict Arnold and Robert Fulton. Next was the residence of Judge Robert R. Livingston, and afterward of his son, Chancellor Livingston. From here Washington viewed the fireworks on his inaugural night. The fourth house, No. 7, the only relic of former times which remains standing in this vicinity, was the interesting home of John Stevens,— the inventor and builder of the first steamship that ever ploughed the ocean. Nos. 9 and 11 were connected houses, afterward converted into the Atlantic Garden, the site of which originally was occupied by the tavern of a Dutch burgomaster, Martin Cregier.

THE WELLES BUILDING, No. 18, stands at the opposite side of the street. Just beyond, at No. 26, is the imposing pile built and occupied by the Standard Oil Company. This edifice, like many of our buildings, possesses no definite style; indeed, the variety that is to be found in nearly every architectural structure in the city may be said to form a composite that is distinctly American,—it being almost impossible to preserve a pure historic style and meet modern requirements.

Aldrich Court, at No. 45, is a sort of modernized Romanesque.

The Consolidated Stock and Petroleum Exchange, at the corner of Exchange Place and Broadway, is a crude conglomeration in design. Visitors are admitted to the gallery of this building, from 10 A.M. until 3 P.M., to watch the buying and selling of oil, mining, and railroad stocks.

No. 41 Broadway is the place where stood the first habitations erected by white men on Manhattan Island. The McComb Mansion occupied the site in later years, where lived the French minister during the early part of the first administration, and where Washington subsequently resided for a few months previous to the removal of the capital to Philadelphia.

Trinity Church.—The conspicuous brown stone edifice which next challenges attention is "Old Trinity," one of the most interesting landmarks in New York, and the established head of the Episcopal church in this country. With the exception of the Dutch Reformed Collegiate Corporation, it is the oldest church organization in the United States,—Episcopacy having become the leading religious system under the royal government. Trinity Church originally was erected in 1696,—a grant of

land having been obtained from William and
Mary, to be located "in or near to a street
without the north gate of the city, commonly
called Broadway." In 1703 the parish was further enriched by Queen Anne with a gift of
the "King's Farm," a district including about
thirty blocks in the immediate vicinity. Because the clergy persisted in reading the
prayer for the king, the church was closed at
the outbreak of the Revolution, and it was
destroyed by fire soon afterward. In 1790 a
new structure was erected, in which a richly
ornamented and canopied pew was dedicated
to the President of the United States, and another was reserved for the Governor of New
York. The second edifice was pulled down in
1839, when the present handsome specimen of
Gothic architecture was erected on its site.

The church doors always stand invitingly
open. Chimes in the belfry chant the hours.
Inside, carved Gothic columns support a
groined roof. The reredos, which is a memorial to William B. Astor, erected by his
sons, is a perfect flower-garden of architectural art, composed of marbles, Caen stones,
and mosaics of glass and precious stones. The
middle panel of the altar is made up of a Maltese cross, in the four arms of which are cut
cameos representing symbols of the Evangel-

ists. while at the intersection of the arms is a
delicately outlined bust of the Saviour. A
ring of lapis lazuli encircles the cross, in which
are set chrysoprase and carbuncles. Rays are
formed of red and white tufa, with gold as an
enrichment, and the whole is framed with a
rich carving of passion flowers. At each side
are kneeling angels, carved in white marble,
framed by red Lisbon marble shafts, with
white marble carved capitals and divisional
bands. The side panels are very beautiful, but
somewhat less elaborate. The carved panels
above the altar line represent scenes in the
life of Christ, the middle one being a fine rendering of Leonardo da Vinci's "Last Supper."
Statuettes of the Apostles, separated by red
granite columns, occupy the next line, with a
large triangular carving of the Crucifixion.
An elaborately carved course of natural foliage, with birds and flowers, forms the cornice, which is broken in the middle by a gable
completed by a plain cross. The four buttresses are surmounted with pinnacles of rich
carving that support angels with uplifted
wings, the treatment being similar to Fra
Angelico. The whole design is in keeping
with the characteristics of the church, the style
being the perpendicular Gothic of the fourteenth, fifteenth, and sixteenth centuries.

The last record of many names illustrious in history may be found in the graveyard surrounding the church. Near the left entrance is the monument to Captain Lawrence. The tomb of Alexander Hamilton is near the Rector Street railing. Just west of it is the vault of Robert Livingston, in which also reposes the body of Robert Fulton. In the northeastern corner is a monument which was erected by Trinity Corporation in honor of the heroes who died in the British prisons. Near by are graves that date back to the first church, and in close proximity to the railing is a flat stone marked "Charlotte Temple," the unfortunate woman whose sad history is told in the novel which bears her name.

Trinity Corporation supports six chapels and numerous parochial schools and charities. It always has been munificent in its liberality to public and private interests. Its property is very valuable, the income derived from it being about half a million dollars per annum.

WALL STREET.—Directly opposite Trinity Church is a street which contains almost as many associations as the localities previously described, even its name having been derived from the fact that a protecting wall, which defined the northern boundary of the city, once followed its course. Elegant residences lined the street in later days, that subsequently gave place to government buildings and the financial institutions that, since the civil war, have become world-famous through the extent of their transactions.

The massive and imposing buildings that now stand at the south side of the street are the United Bank Building, at the corner of Broadway, No. 13, the visitors' entrance to the Stock Exchange,—one of the chief places of interest to strangers,—open from nine to three o'clock daily, the Drexel Building, at the corner of Nassau Street, the Mills Building, adjoining the Drexel Building in Broad Street, several very ornate buildings that belong to banking concerns, and the United States Custom House,—a granite structure with a portico containing eighteen Ionic columns thirty-eight feet in height. The rotunda of this building is eighty feet high, the dome of which is supported by eight pilasters of fine variegated Italian marble. The departments connected with the Custom House are those of the Collector, the Naval Officer, the Surveyor, and the Deputy Surveyor,—who is in charge of the Barge Office at the Battery.

In 1709 a slave-market was instituted at the foot of Wall Street, at which time Africans were brought to the city in large numbers.

No. 46, at the north side of the street, is the spot identified with the office where Professor Morse's telegraphic instrument and one operator long remained idle while waiting for the recognition of the commercial world. The handsome block of granite near by is utilized entirely for business offices.

THE UNITED STATES ASSAY OFFICE, where visitors may see the preparation of gold and silver bullion daily, between the hours of 10 A.M. and 2 P.M., is easily identified, being the oldest building in the vicinity.

THE UNITED STATES SUB-TREASURY, at the corner of Nassau Street, is a building associated with so much of our history that a short digression becomes necessary.

During the administration of the third Dutch Governor, Kieft, a clumsy stone house was erected in Pearl Street for the purpose of accommodating travellers, public meetings, and later, a public school. Afterward, when the house was remodelled, and a pillory, cage, whipping-post and ducking-stool were added to its accommodations, it was called the "Stadt-Huys," or City Hall, and remained in active use until 1700, when a new City Hall was built upon the site of the present Sub-Treasury,— the ground having been a gift to the city from Colonel Abraham De Peyster, who was mayor in 1691. Besides the rooms necessarily devoted to public business in this later edifice, one afterward contained the Corporation Library, a gift to the city of one thousand six hundred and twenty two volumes; another was used as a fire-engine house, while the entire upper story became converted into a Debtor's Prison. From the balcony was read the Declaration of Independence, July 18th, 1776, amidst the

rapturous applause of citizens who understood the fierce struggle it inaugurated. After the war, when Congress appropriated the building, it was remodeled by private subscription into the Federal Hall, where Washington was unanimously elected President of the new Republic, where he was inaugurated, April 30th, 1789, and where Congress met while New York was the Capital of the Nation.

The subsequent rapid growth of the city necessitating a new City Hall as early as 1812, the Government purchased Federal Hall and erected the present structure on its site, intending it originally for a Custom House. This granite edifice is of Doric design, having a portico containing marble columns thirty-two feet in height. Through holes in the ceiling of the portico balls may be dropped should the building be attacked by a mob.

THE COLOSSAL STATUE OF "WASHINGTON TAKING THE OATH OF OFFICE," by J. Q. A. Ward, which stands at the entrance, is an admirable work of art, erected by the New York Chamber of Commerce and presented to the United States Government in 1883, President Arthur accepting the gift in behalf of the Government just one hundred years after Washington's triumphal entry into New York. Near the base of the statue lies the identical stone upon which Washington stood during the ceremony of the first inauguration.

Within the building, to which visitors are

admitted from 10 A.M. until 3 P.M., are many vaults for the storage of coins and notes. Desks of the different divisions surround the rotunda, the dome of which is supported by sixteen Corinthian columns cut from solid blocks of marble.

The last object of prominence in the street is the Astor Building, at No. 10.

LOWER BROADWAY AND VICINITY FROM WALL STREET TO THE POST-OFFICE. — At the west side of Broadway, one block north of Trinity Church, stands a building which was erected by, and bears the name of, Francis Boreel, a Dutch nobleman who married the granddaughter of John Jacob Astor. The spot on which this building stands originally was occupied by the elegant home of Lieutenant-Governor James De Lancey, after whose death the property was converted into a public house, known by a great variety of names, the most famous of which was "Burns' Coffee House." In this hotel the celebrated "Non-Importation Agreement" was signed. Later, the house became a favorite resort of the British officers, on account of its proximity to "The Mall,"—a fashionable promenade in front of Trinity Church,—and after the Revolution its "great room" was the scene of Washington's inauguration ball; also of many public dinners, concerts, and assemblies. In 1793 a syndicate of New York merchants pulled down the old building and erected a new one, called the City Hotel, which furnished accommodations for the entertainment of magnates, as well as for public assemblies of every description.

At the opposite side of the street is the Guernsey Building, No. 164. The Equitable Life Insurance Building, on the same side of the way, between Pine and Cedar Streets, is an excellent specimen of modern French Renaissance. The interior contains a magnificent court, filled with offices and stalls. In the wall near the stairway is a fine mosaic. The story occupied by the Equitable Life Insurance Company is magnificently decorated with marble. A Signal Service Station may be investigated at the top of the building, and the Safe Deposit Vaults in the basement are open to inspection.

CHAPTER II.

THE FIRST AFTERNOON.

The court of the Equitable Building leads to Nassau Street, where stands a splendid granite structure, erected by the Mutual Life Insurance Company, in modern French Renaissance style.

THE HISTORIC MIDDLE DUTCH CHURCH, of quaint Holland architecture, which formerly occupied the site of the last mentioned building, was erected in 1729. Here twelve elders with stereotyped countenances sat in solemn state around the high pulpit, and listened to the Dutch dominies whose learned discourses were delivered in their native tongue until 1764. It was in the wooden steeple of this church that Franklin experimented with the lightning. The bell, a gift from Colonel Abraham De Peyster, was cast in Amsterdam, where many citizens are said to have thrown silver coins into the metal while it was in fusion. During the Revolution the church was used by the English for a prison, three thousand Federal troops having endured incredible sufferings within its walls, while almost as many more were confined in an old sugarhouse near by. In 1844 the property was sold to the Government, when for a number of

THE POST-OFFICE IN THE NASSAU STREET CHURCH.

years it was used as a post-office. The old bell is now placed in front of the church at the corner of Fifth Avenue and 29th Street.

A fine building, owned by the Library Corporation, and containing the earliest loan-library in America,—since removed to the corner of Leonard Street and Broadway,—once stood at the corner of Nassau and Cedar Streets.

Nassau, one of the oldest streets in New

York, still retains the narrow irregularity of the foot-path which gave it its direction. Maiden Lane, which crosses Nassau Street one block north of the Insurance Building, is now a trade-centre for manufacturing jewellers, but was once a favorite resort for laundresses, on account of the little stream which flowed through it,—hence its name, "Maagde paetze," or "Virgin's path." In John Street, one block further north, was a small wooden theatre, called the Theatre Royal, in which British officers often were amateur performers, and where Major André was both amateur actor and scene-painter. In 1786 the first Methodist church was erected in this street.

"THE RUSSIAN WEDDING FEAST," a celebrated painting by Makoffsky, is exhibited at No. 24 John Street. In this picture the artist has portrayed the moment when a young husband is about to salute his blushing bride,—for the first time unveiled before him,—while the guests are waiting until this part of the ceremony shall have been performed before they drink to the health of the young couple. The figures are animated, the faces expressive, and the costumes and decorations superb. The grouping of endless varieties of color into a perfectly harmonious whole is the most noticeable feature of this painting. An entrance fee of twenty-five cents, which is appropriated to some charitable institution, is charged.

At the corner of Broadway and Dey Street, directly opposite John Street, is the Western Union Telegraph Company Building, the design of which is sometimes called Neo-Grec. The Coal and Iron Exchange is one block south, at No. 19 Cortland Street.

Fulton, the first street north of Dey and John Streets, is known by the same name from one river to the other. Washington Market is at the Hudson River terminus, and Fulton Market is in the same street, near the East River. The region of the last named place of merchandise was once called "Golden Hill." A skirmish at Cliff and Fulton Streets in January 1770,—caused by the indignation which the British soldiers aroused by repeatedly demolishing the liberty poles erected by citizens, —has been termed the first battle of the Revolution. In this first, as in the last conflict, the British were worsted.

The southeastern corner of Fulton Street and Broadway is occupied by the *Evening Post* Building.

ST. PAUL'S CHAPEL, the next attraction in Broadway, was built in 1766 by Trinity Corporation, and is the oldest church edifice in the city. Trinity Congregation has occupied this chapel several times while its own edifice was in process of reconstruction. Here divine service was conducted in 1789, immediately after the inauguration of Washington, and also in 1889, at the centennial celebration of that event. During the early part of his administration the first President worshipped in the pew which is situated under the gallery at the northern side of the chapel, about half-way between the chancel and the vestry, and adorned by a fresco of the American Eagle. Governor George Clinton occupied the pew directly opposite.

The churchyard adds to the venerable appearance of the chapel. Under the portico, at the Broadway side, lie the remains of General Richard Montgomery, who was killed in 1775 while storming Quebec, and on the wall above is a tablet erected to his memory by order of Congress. At the left stands a monument to Thomas Addis Emmet,—the brilliant Irish patriot who came to America soon after his release from imprisonment in Ireland, and established himself here in the practice of law. Dr. Mac Nevin, Emmet's compatriot and fellow-sufferer, has a monument at the right. The actor, George Frederick Cooke, is also buried in these grounds. The rector and vestry of Trinity Church occupy offices in the building at the rear of the cemetery.

The block at the north of the chapel is occupied by the Astor House. The *New York Herald* Building is at the southeastern corner of Broadway and Ann Street, where, in former years, P. T. Barnum drew large crowds to visit his American Museum.

THE POST-OFFICE.—The triangular building opposite the Astor House is the city Post-Office, completed in 1877. The material is of light-colored granite, and the architecture is a mixture of Doric and Renaissance, the domes having been patterned after those of the Louvre in Paris. The third and fourth floors are occupied by the Law Institute and Library, and by the United States Courts and their offices, but the remainder of the building is used entirely by the Post-Office Department. Eight hundred million letters, newspapers, etc., are delivered annually. From twelve to twenty collections are daily made from sixteen hundred lamp-post boxes, and over two thousand men are employed in the main office and the seventeen sub-stations under its control. Although the postal facilities of the present office are admirable, its capacity is not sufficient for the constantly increasing business of our rapidly growing city. The question of a larger building, to be located very much further north, is now agitating the public mind.

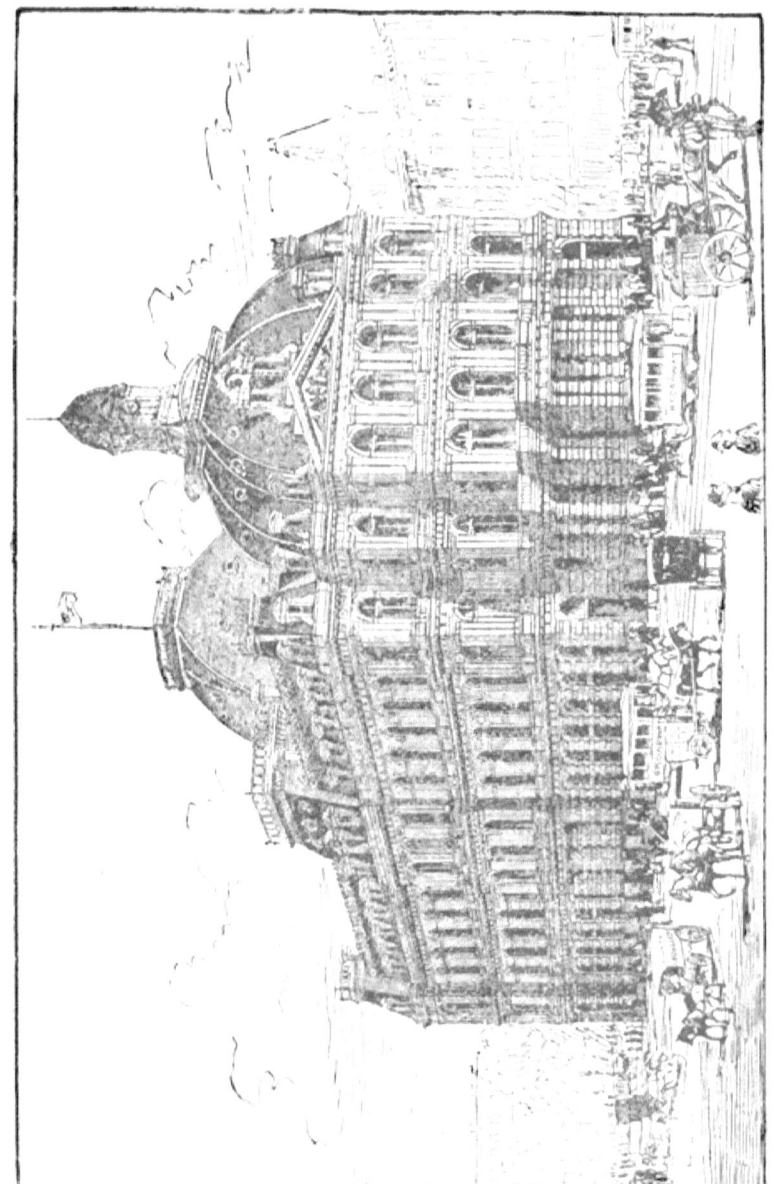

THE NEW YORK CITY POST-OFFICE.

In former years, before the Middle Dutch Church was used as a post-office, a rotunda in the park north of the present building, was changed from a cyclorama to a station for the distribution of Uncle Sam's mail. The indignation of the merchants was at this time aroused because the post-office was located so far up-town.

In 1718 the first rope-walk appeared in Broadway, between Barclay Street and Park Place.

Columbia College, originally called King's College, formerly stood west of Broadway, in Park Place.

CITY HALL PARK.—The park at the north of the Post Office was called "The Fields," or "The Commons," in the early days, the ground now occupied by the Post-Office having been included. At a public meeting in this place Alexander Hamilton delivered his maiden speech.

The white marble building designed in the Italian style of architecture is the City Hall. At the time of its completion in 1812, it was unsurpassed by any edifice in the country; indeed it was the only chaste and classic specimen of architecture which New York possessed until the pure Gothic of Trinity and Grace Churches inspired a desire for something better than the feeble imitations of Greek temples that previously had abounded. The headquarters of the city government are in this building; also the city library. The "Governors' Room" contains portraits of national celebrities, the chairs used by the first Con-

THE CITY HALL.

gress, the desk on which Washington penned his first message to Congress, and his inaugural chair. Here the remains of President Lincoln were laid in state, while for twenty-four hours a sad procession, which even during the night did not diminish in volume, surged by him.

THE COUNTY COURT HOUSE stands at the northern end of the park, a white marble building of Corinthian design, which perpetuates the memory of the gigantic frauds that occurred during the Tweed *régime*. Different authorities estimate the cost of this edifice to the city to have been from eight to thirty millions of dollars. It now accommodates the State Courts and several of the city departments. The city almshouse formerly stood on this site.

A jail, called "The Provost," which previous to the Revolution had been erected near the eastern border of the park, was used during the British occupation for the confinement of notable American prisoners, the marshal making himself conspicuous for his criminal treatment of the captives. This relic of Revolutionary times still stands. After the war it was used as a debtors' prison, common felons having been confined in the "Bridewell," which stood between the City Hall and Broadway. A gallows frowned between the two buildings. In 1830 "Provost" was remodelled to imitate the Temple of Diana at Ephesus, and has since been used for the offices of the Register, except when during the cholera scourge of 1832 it was converted temporarily into a hospital.

PARK ROW.—Because the group of lofty buildings that face the park from the east and south are mostly newspaper offices, the place has received the name of "Printing House Square." The huge structures that stand a little to the south of the park are provided with law and business offices. Temple Court, at the southwestern corner of Nassau and Beekman Streets, is one hundred and sixty feet in height. The Morse Building, at the northeastern corner of the same streets, is one hundred and sixty-five feet in height. The Potter Building, opposite, at the northwestern corner, is one hundred and eighty-five feet, and the *Times* Building, just north of this, is two hundred and thirteen feet The material of this last named edifice is light granite, and its style is a beautiful adaptation of the Gothic. The *Tribune* Building, which was the first lofty edifice in this vicinity, stands at the corner of Spruce Street and Park Row, with a bronze statue of its founder, Horace Greeley, on the sidewalk in front of one of its windows. The *Sun* Building is next to the *Tribune* Building, while at the north, towering over all, is the Pulitzer Building, a colossus of the colossi, of Scotch sandstone and terra-cotta, three hundred and seventy-five feet in height. Visitors are freely admitted to the dome of this building (from whence the vision extends over forty-five miles of country), and to the *World* offices and press-room. The twelfth floor contains the best appointed composing-room in the world. On the numerous floors above are the editorial, reportorial, and photo-engraving rooms. The distributing-room is in the basement, and the press-room occupies the cellar. In this latter apartment are eight cylinder presses connected with machines that cut and fold the papers ready for delivery. To watch these mighty servants of civilization at their work is most entertaining. The design of this majestic edifice is a free treatment of the Romanesque.

On the site of these gigantic structures formerly were the "Brick Church" (Presbyterian), of which the popular Dr. Spring was pastor, and the Park Theatre, a play-house where the best society witnessed histrionic exhibitions by Matthews, Cooper, Cooke, Kean, Macready, and Junius Brutus Booth.

THE STATUE OF AMERICA'S PHILOSOPHER AND PATRIOT, BENJAMIN FRANKLIN, by Plassman, which stands in the Square, was given to the city by a private citizen in 1872.

FRANKLIN SQUARE.—A short walk in Frankfort Street, an unattractive thoroughfare south of the Pulitzer Building, affords an opportunity for inspecting the supporting-towers of Brooklyn Bridge, the arches under the bridge-approach, etc. The elevated-railroad station, which crosses the street at Franklin Square, marks a spot once celebrated for its aristocratic residences. The first presidential mansion was in Cherry Street, near Pearl, but proved to be inconvenient because so far out of town. Walton House, the palace of the city, was at No. 326 Pearl Street, the grounds extending eastward to the river. Harpers' Publishing House is the only object of interest in the vicinity now, business and tenement houses having obliterated all traces of former grandeur.

THE MODEL TENEMENT HOUSES erected by a company composed of members of the Society for Ethical Culture, are some distance beyond, at No. 306 Cherry Street. The houses are kept in excellent repair, and yield four and one-half per cent. on the investment, the object of the company being to realize a fair profit and not an exorbitant one. From Franklin Square to South Street is but a step; there the Belt Line cars run northeast to Montgomery Street, near which, in Cherry Street, these houses are situated. Returning, the cars at the corner of East Broadway and Essex Street will convey passengers to Broadway at Ann Street.

BROOKLYN BRIDGE.—East of City Hall Park is Brooklyn Suspension Bridge, over which about ninety-eight thousand persons daily pass. The entire length of the bridge is five thousand, nine hundred and and eighty-nine feet, and its width is eighty-five feet, including a promenade for foot-passengers, two railroad tracks—on which run passenger cars propelled by a stationary engine on the Brooklyn side—and two roadways for vehicles. The floor of the bridge at its greatest height is one hundred and thirty-five feet above high-water mark, but full-rigged ships have to strike their topgallant masts to pass under unimpeded. The height above water of the supporting towers is two hundred and seventy-two feet. The bridge was opened in the summer of 1883, having been constructed at a cost of fifteen millions of dollars. A ride over the railway to Brooklyn, returning by way of the promenade, will afford the best views of the bridge, the East River, and the Bay.

LOWER BROADWAY.—The yellow surface cars that pass the City Hall Park at the west furnish the best means of viewing Broadway from this point to 14th Street.

The white marble building at the Chambers Street corner, formerly was A. T. Stewart's

BROOKLYN BRIDGE.

wholesale dry-goods store, but is now remodelled for offices. The site originally was used as a negro burial-ground. Two blocks further north Duane Street marks the site of the old New York City Hospital, built in 1775, and surrounded by five acres of ground containing magnificent elms. The Ionic Building at Leonard Street belongs to the New York Life Insurance Company. At this place Contoit's Garden used to call together the fashionable people, young and old, to enjoy its cool shade, and partake of its ices and lemonades. The magnificent building of the Globe Mutual Life Insurance Company is directly opposite.

CANAL STREET, so called because a canal which formed an outlet for the waters of Collect Pond once ran through it to the Hudson River, is a little further north. Sidewalks and roadways were on each side of the water,— which explains the width of the street,—and a stone bridge crossed it at Broadway. When the canal was filled in this bridge was left intact, and still remains imbedded under the pavement.

THE BOARD OF EDUCATION occupies a building at the right of Broadway, in Grand Street, No. 146.

NIBLO'S GARDEN THEATRE, at the Prince Street corner, is very spacious and pleasing, the stage usually being devoted to spectacular plays. Both the theatre and the adjoining Metropolitan Hotel belong to the estate of the late A. T. Stewart.

RICHMOND HILL, the delightful country seat where General and Mrs. Washington were quartered during the eventful summer of 1776, was situated west of this, near the Hudson. Afterward, when it was the home of the first vice-president, Mrs. Adams wrote of it: "In natural beauty it might vie with the most delicious spot I ever saw." It was the residence of Aaron Burr at the time of his duel with Hamilton, but was soon after sold to John Jacob Astor, who converted it into a public resort.

THE CENTRAL POLICE STATION is the next point of interest near which the car passes. It is situated in Mulberry Street, two blocks east of Broadway, and one-half block north of Houston Street. In it is exhibited the "Rogues' Gallery," a collection of more than a thousand photographs of notorious criminals. The police force of the city consists of three thousand, two hundred men. There are thirty-five precincts,—one of which includes the harbor,—each under the command of a captain and sergeants. Each precinct has a building for the accommodation of policemen and homeless individuals.

A City Shop.—No visit to the city would be complete without inspecting some of the leading shops, and probably none of them have so many interesting associations as the extensive dry-goods house which occupies the entire block between 9th and 10th Streets, in Broadway. This is now known by the firm name of Hilton, Hughes & Denning, but it was A. T. Stewart who secured for the establishment its notoriety. There has been no especial change in the interior since the death of the founder, except that which is demanded by changing fashions. In the well-lighted rotunda, with its elaborate decoration of stucco work, just as rich fabrics are displayed, and each of the different departments is as complete as when under the rule of the merchant who made himself a prince and his place of business a palace.

Below stairs are ceramics, bric-à-brac, and household goods. The main floor is occupied with dry-goods, while the floors above contain carpets, artistic furniture, and reception rooms. The unique feature of this shop at present is its display of the statuary which formerly adorned the home of Mr. Stewart. While a promiscuous pile of dry-goods is not the best background for these gems of sculptured art, it certainly is a privilege to see them.

The statue of Proserpine, Marshall Wood, sculptor, is near Broadway, at the 9th Street side. "The Bather," by Tantardine, is near the 9th Street elevator. An exquisite conception of Sappho, by Crawford, faces the rotunda near by. A much less effective piece of Crawford's work is the "Flora" which stands in the 9th Street and Fourth Avenue corner. A fine bust of Washington, by Hiram Powers, faces the rotunda at the Fourth Avenue side, and near the 10th Street staircase is Harriet Hosmer's noble rendering of "Zenobia in Chains." A most interesting study of Demosthenes, by Crawford, is placed near the 10th Street elevator. "Paul and Virginia," by Joseph Dunham, and John Randolph Rogers' "Blind Nydia Fleeing from Pompeii" are close by, completing the list, with the exception of a "Fisher Girl" by Tadolini, which stands in a reception room upstairs. The one object missing from the valuable collection is Hiram Powers' "Greek Slave."

The Studio Building in West 10th Street, near Sixth Avenue, has for many years been the home of our most celebrated artists. Near by is the Jefferson Market court and prison, an irregular but unique and handsome structure, built of red brick and sandstone, in the Italian Gothic style. Adjoining this is Jefferson Market, a brick structure richly ornamented with terra-cotta.

GRACE CHURCH.—In Broadway, north of Denning's, stands Grace Church, which, with the edifices attached, is built of white limestone, in chaste, fourteenth century Gothic style, forming one of the most beautiful architectural effects in the city. The rectory is connected with the church by a clergy-house, which contains a library and reading-room open to church members. In the grounds is a colossal terra-cotta jar that was found forty feet below the surface in Rome. The small building at the south of the church is the chantry, in which daily services are held. This, with the chancel, and two organs connected by electrical machinery, are gifts from Miss Catharine Lorillard Wolfe, the chancel having been erected as a memorial to her father. The tower contains a fine set of chimes. Back of the church, in Fourth Avenue, is a day-nursery for the reception of young children during the hours when their mothers are at work. This is known as Grace Memorial Home, and was erected by Vice-President Levi P. Morton as a tribute to his wife.

Grace Church was founded in 1805, its first building occupying the corner of Broadway and Rector Street. The present structure was built in 1846. Next to Trinity, Grace is the wealthiest Episcopal church corporation in the city.

The Star Theatre, at the corner of 13th Street, was built in 1862, and shortly afterward came under the able management of Lester Wallack, who for twenty years associated its boards with all that is best in legitimate comedy. The management changed when Wallack's new theatre was opened, but the place retains its prestige, and good plays are always presented.

CHAPTER III.

THE SECOND MORNING.

"AFTER THE HUNT," by W. M. Harnett.— A remarkable painting on exhibition at No. 8 Warren Street, represents an old barn door on which hang implements of the chase and trophies of a hunt. Probably nothing more realistic ever has been seen on canvas than these panels, so marvellously like wood, in which a cunningly wrought nail-hole deceives the most practised eye. The glint of brass surrounding the lock, the sheen of the mother-of-pearl on the stock of the old gun, and the metal and old cracked bone in the hilt of the sword, decoy nearly every one into emphatic assertions that the work is inlaid and not painted. The drawing in this picture is exceptionally fine. A battle scene in the Franco-Prussian war, and "The Quarrel," by Meissonier, are in the collection of paintings here exhibited. Although these pictures are in a saloon, ladies are frequent visitors between the hours of eight and eleven A.M.

The Staats Zeitung Building, over the portals of which stand life-size bronze statues of Franklin and Gutenberg, is across the park, at the junction of Park Row and Centre Street. This, in the old days, was the starting point of the Boston Road.

CHATHAM STREET.—From the *Staats Zeitung* Building to Chatham Square, Park Row, formerly called Chatham Street, has long been inhabited by Jews who deal in cheap clothing. The Newsboys' Lodging-house is east of Park Row, in the first street which crosses it. From one room in a private house in this vicinity the first post-office distributed mail to the city. At the right, in Madison Street, near Pearl Street, the first public school opened in 1805, with forty pupils, De Witt Clinton and the Society of Friends having been instrumental in projecting a work which is now expanded until it comprises three hundred schools and a free college under a municipal Board of Education. At the northwestern corner of Park Row and Baxter Street the famous Tea-water Pump was situated,—a remarkable spring from which fourteen thousand and three hundred gallons of pure water were daily drawn, and sold about town for one penny a gallon.

CHATHAM SQUARE, which is but two blocks from Baxter Street, was formerly the burial-ground of the Jews. Just beyond were the British intrenchments, in which dead bodies of American prisoners were indiscriminately thrown without rites of sepulture.

THE FIVE POINTS.—At the west, Worth Street leads by Mulberry and Baxter Streets, where are teeming masses of the lowest grades of humanity. The junction which is formed by Baxter with other streets is called "The Five Points,"—a locality long celebrated for the criminal character of its population, but now reclaimed, through the efforts of devoted missionaries, until its dangerous elements have nearly disappeared. Italians, Chinese, beggars, boot-blacks, opium-peddlers, etc., live in the vicinity now, but criminals are rare. An old brewery, which once sheltered the very worst characters and was associated with the most appalling crimes, is no more, and the low dens that still are to be found in the narrow streets near by will rapidly be obliterated by the business houses that continually are encroaching. A visit to one of the missions at least should not be omitted.

THE FIVE POINTS "HOUSE OF INDUSTRY," founded in 1850, has since that time received over twenty thousand inmates and furnished instruction to forty thousand children. *Gamins* from the neighborhood, as well as those

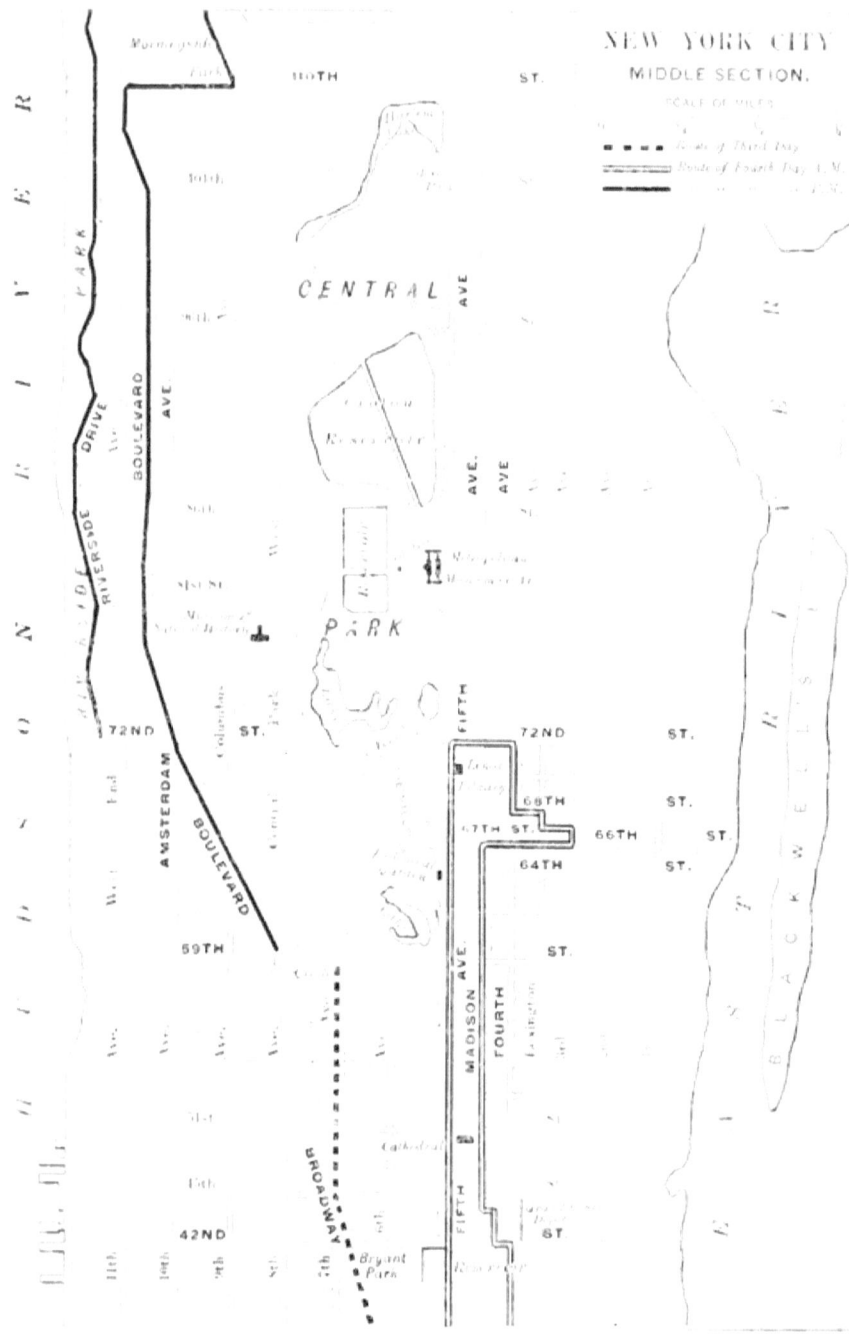

children who reside in the building, are carefully trained in common school branches, special attention being given to the study of the physiological effects of alcohol. A daily bath also exercises its salutary influence upon the pupils. A children's song-service, composed of classical selections astonishingly well rendered,—and demonstrating the practicability of utilizing the best music as a means of refining the ignorant,—is held Sunday afternoons at half-past three o'clock, after which visitors are permitted to inspect the building. The officers of the institution, who keep themselves informed concerning the welfare of the children that have been under their care, assert that so far only two have been known to lead criminal lives. Women also are here sheltered, and employment is found for them.

"The Five Points Mission" is opposite, and in the small space between is a band-stand, where open-air evening concerts are given to audiences composed of tramps and drunkards of both sexes, whose faces expose their hardened characters, making the name of the place, Paradise Park, an awful misnomer.

THE TOMBS.—In Centre Street, one block toward the west, stands an imposing granite pile, ominously called "The Tombs," and used as the city prison. This edifice, which covers

an entire block, was erected in 1838 on ground
made by filling Collect Pond. Although the
foundations of the building were laid much
deeper than usual, the walls settled and appeared to be in peril, but as they have stood
for over half a century, they are now consid-

THE TOMBS

ered safe. The site chosen was unfortunate,
because the hollow ground does not show the
really fine building,—which is said to be the
purest specimen of Egyptian architecture out
of Egypt,—to advantage, and also because the
necessarily damp and unwholesome condition
of the soil renders the place a very poor one

for the confinement of human beings. To further add to the pestilential condition of this swamp-land, some tanners, who previously occupied the locality, left their vats open when they removed their tanneries, and for a long time these plague-spots remained unrectified.

In the portico massive and sombre pillars, well calculated to induce a hopeless state of mind, lead to the Court of Special Sessions and the Police Court, both of which may be visited without permits from 9.30 A.M. until 4 P.M. The prison entrance is in Franklin Street. Here criminals wait to be tried and convicts were executed. Permits are required in order to visit the dark and gloomy cells between the hours of 11 A.M. and 2 P.M. These may be secured from the Commissioners of Public Charities and Correction, at their bureau, corner of Third Avenue and 11th Street.

A new building for the accommodation of the criminal courts is in process of construction at the north of the prison.

MOTT STREET.—Returning to Chatham Square by Worth Street a few moments should be devoted to Mott Street, which swarms with representatives of the Chinese nation, usually very well-behaved persons. The Joss houses are easily discoverable because of their oriental decorations, but they are not open to the public. The exclusively foreign aspect of the place inspires one with the feeling of the child who, when taken to visit the panorama of Gettysburg, asked, "Why, where is New York?"

THE BOWERY.—From Chatham Square the up-town train on the elevated road passes through a street which bears the most unique of reputations. "The Bowery" from beginning to end is a queer conglomeration of cheap stores, concert-saloons, variety theatres, and dime museums, while venders of all sorts of small wares impede the sidewalks. The character of this locality also has changed with time. The "Bowery Boy," who terrorized the police, and made his face good for an entrance-fee to the theatre, has disappeared; and even the "young fellow" of the period finds his paste diamonds too little appreciated by the Germans, who are rapidly taking possession of his old "stamping ground." The name of this street was derived from the fact that it originally was a lane passing by Dutch farms or "booweries."

THE OLD BOWERY THEATRE, the history of which is closely interwoven with traditions of the American stage, still stands below Canal Street. Malibran, Hackett, Forrest, the elder Booth, Charlotte Cushman, and many other great stars, have made this place luminous with their presence. Since their day the rougher class has made it a home for heterogeneous melodrama.

Three savings banks in this street have greatly aided to promote frugal habits among residents of the vicinity. A branch of the Young Men's Christian Association is also located here. The shopping centre for country people and the smaller trades-people is east, in Grand Street, where goods are much cheaper than in the fashionable quarter. A totally different aspect characterizes this locality from that which appears about the up-town stores.

At East 3d Street it will again be necessary to become a pedestrian.

LAFAYETTE PLACE, which extends at right angles with East 3d, or Great Jones Street, one block west of the Bowery, is a quarter in which the antiquated style of the old residences,—now mostly appropriated by publishing houses, religious newspapers, hotels, and restaurants,—has given them an air of great respectability.

THE ASTOR LIBRARY BUILDING, at the east side of the street, covering the site of the old Vauxhall Garden, is of brown-stone and brick, Romanesque in design, and in pattern similar to the royal palaces of Florence. This edifice was erected in 1853,—according to the will of John Jacob Astor,—who left four hundred thousand dollars for this purpose; and appointed the most able scholars, with Washington Irving as their president, to act as trustees. There are now about three hundred thousand books on the shelves, mainly books of reference, and the fact that annually there are about sixty thousand persons who seek exact knowledge in this classic library demonstrates the intelligence of the age. There is still capacity for about two hundred thousand volumes. In the collection are records of the effective work of the United States Sanitary Commission during the war, rare Greek and Latin manuscripts, an illuminated manuscript volume of chants used at the coronation of French kings, and some black-letter tomes that include a copy of the first printed Bible, and a fair amount of Shakesperiana. These will be shown on application. The library is open from 9 A.M. to 5 P.M., and is accessible to any person by simply registering name and address. Since the original endowment, William B. Astor has contributed five hundred and fifty thousand dollars, and John Jacob Astor,—the grandson of the founder,—three hundred thousand dollars.

On its departure for Washington in 1861,

THE ASTOR LIBRARY.

the Seventh Regiment National Guard formed in line along this street, amid great excitement and a profuse display of banners and bunting. This corps was composed of the youth and flower of the city.

CHAPTER IV.

THE SECOND AFTERNOON.

THE MERCANTILE LIBRARY.—Astor Place, which diagonally crosses Lafayette Place at the north, is a quarter mostly occupied by publishing houses. A new Clinton Hall stands at the triangle formed by the junction of Astor Place and 8th Street, the old one which stood on the same site having recently been pulled down because it was too small to accommodate the Mercantile Library, for which it had long been a home. This library, founded in 1821 for merchants' clerks, occupied a hall (called Clinton Hall because De Witt Clinton presented the first book) at the corner of Beekman and Nassau Streets. Columbia College granted two free scholarships to the organization, and members secured many privileges in the way of lecture courses and class instruction. Nothing is more interesting than a history of the institutions founded in this city during the first half-century of our Republic, at which time the energy and insight of a few public-spirited men,—among whom none were more conspicuous than De Witt Clinton,—laid the foundation for broad and far-reaching educational systems that are proving of incalculable benefit to the whole nation. The library was moved to its present site in 1854, and now again has required more commodious quarters. Two hundred thousand volumes, besides newspapers and periodicals, occupy its shelves, and new books are constantly being purchased. Branch libraries are at No. 62 Liberty Street, and at No. 431 Fifth Avenue. The charges for yearly membership are four dollars for clerks, and five dollars for other persons.

The Clinton Hall, which recently has been demolished, originally was the Astor Place Opera House, where in 1849, the Forrest-Macready riot occurred,—an outbreak which was occasioned by the unpopularity of Macready, who was supposed to have prejudiced English opinion against Forrest, the American favorite. A poorly modelled bronze statue of Samuel S. Cox recently has been placed in the triangular space east of Clinton Hall.

COOPER UNION.—The massive brown-stone building at the right, the old portion of which is classic, and the additions of which are Gothic in design, is a monument of far-sighted philanthropy, built in 1857 by the late Peter Cooper, at a cost of six hundred and thirty thousand dollars, and endowed by him with three hundred thousand dollars for the support of the library, free reading-room, and schools

COOPER UNION.

of art and science. The library, which is open between the hours of 8 A.M and 10 P.M. on week days, and on Sundays, from October to May, from 12 M. to 9 P.M., contains a complete set of Patent-Office reports, about twenty thousand books, and the periodicals and newspapers of the day. An average of seventeen hundred persons daily patronize the reading-room, and the annual attendance at the evening schools is thirty-five hundred. Free popular lectures are given Saturday evenings.

A special art school is provided for women during the day, as well as classes in telegraphy, phonography, and typewriting. The large hall of this establishment, which is used for mass meetings, has been identified with almost every public movement since the erection of the building. Its walls have echoed to the clarion voices of Garrison, Beecher, Phillips, Sumner, Anna Dickinson, Lucretia Mott, and Abraham Lincoln,—on the occasion of his presidential campaign against Douglas, the "Little Giant of Illinois."

THE BIBLE HOUSE, just north of Cooper Union, contains the offices of the American Bible Society, an organization whose presses have printed the Bible in eighty languages.

THE SIXTY-NINTH REGIMENT ARMORY is over Tompkins Market, east of Cooper Union. The mention of this regiment still recalls to many minds one of the most harrowing sights of the Civil War, when after the battle of Bull Run, only three hundred members returned from that wholesale massacre, and these came hatless, coatless, and stockingless. The distress of the women who discovered that their loved ones were missing, and the frantic eagerness with which the soldiers grasped their wives and children, is spoken of as a scene affecting in the extreme.

TOMPKINS SQUARE.—From this point St. Mark's Place, or East 8th Street, leads to a pretty park which invites occupants of the tenement houses near by to enjoy the fresh air. Whatever may be the shortcomings of our municipal government no complaint can be made with regard to the floral display, for beautiful little patches of color, arranged with really artistic skill, adorn the public grounds in all parts of the city. In the park just mentioned a fine fountain and ample pond sustain such rare water-exotics as the lotus of Egypt and India, the Egyptian papyrus, South American pond-lilies, and many other varieties of water plants, all of which are catalogued on a signboard. A band-stand, confectionery-booths, and plenty of benches, further indicate the comfort given to the tired working people summer evenings.

THE WILSON INDUSTRIAL SCHOOL FOR GIRLS, which faces the park at the 8th Street corner, is an institution in which the Kitchen Garden System (little girls cooking and arranging tables to a song accompaniment) is in practical operation. The matron of this establishment, Miss Emily Huntington, is the founder of the system.

ST. MARK'S CHURCH.—From Cooper Union Stuyvesant Street leads the traveller past a quaint church edifice which was erected in 1793 by Trinity Corporation, the ground and four thousand dollars in money having been a gift from a great-grandson of Peter Stuyvesant. The remains of the Dutch governor are interred in a vault within the church, having been removed from the chapel which he had previously built upon the site of the present edifice. The original tablet on the outside of the eastern wall indicates his place of sepulcher.

A graveyard surrounds St. Mark's, in which only flat stones mark the resting-place of the dead. From this place the remains of A. T. Stewart were stolen.

SECOND AVENUE.—The broad thoroughfare which cuts off Stuyvesant Street at this point is a portion of Second Avenue that was another fashionable quarter of the olden time, but is now largely occupied by medical and benevolent institutions.

THE NEW YORK HISTORICAL SOCIETY BUILDING at the southeastern corner of 11th Street and Second Avenue, is the receptacle of a large and valuable collection of historical curiosities. This society was organized in 1804 by prominent citizens; "For the collecting and preserving of whatever might relate to the natural, civil and ecclesiastical history of the United States in general, and the great and sovereign State of New York in particular." Material with which to form a "Museum of American Antiquities" was so rapidly secured as to necessitate several removals, until the present building was erected with accommodations so spacious that the society enlarged the scope of its work and purchased valuable collections of foreign art, literature, and antiquity. These are now so numerous as to render the present building inadequate for their accommodation, and it is discreditable to the city that so many old treasures should be hidden from the public for want of space, of cases to protect, custodians to exhibit, or catalogues to assist the investigator. The museum contains a large collection of rare pamphlets and manuscripts relating to American history, newspapers, maps, autograph letters, coins, medals, a library of over two thousand volumes, the original portraits of fourteen Inca monarchs, with their names and the order of their succession, and some portraits of celebrated Indian chiefs. The original water-color pictures made by Audubon for his work on natural history are here; also the efforts of the early American artists, West, Allston, Stuart, Peale, Jarvis, Cole and others; and some specimens from the old masters, Raphael, Van Dyke,

Titian, Rembrandt, Del Sarto, Paul Veronese, and Murillo. The Egyptian collection contains a fac-simile of the Rosetta Stone, mummies of the sacred bulls, with portions of the chariot and rope-harness found buried with them in the tombs at Dashour, vases, agricultural and sacrificial implements, and a great number of other equally interesting relics from that ancient civilization. There are besides some specimens of the sculpture of ancient Nineveh, as well as several pieces of modern times.

The society includes over two thousand members, through whose courtesy alone admittance to the building is obtained. As the organization is unincumbered by debt, it is confidently hoped that a new building soon will be erected which can be utilized for the benefit of the public.

STUYVESANT SQUARE, through which Second Avenue passes on its way northward, is one of the most attractive of our city parks, the land for which was deeded to the "Mayor, Aldermen, and Commonalty of the City of New York" (this is our legal title) by Peter G. Stuyvesant in 1836. The donor intended that the park should be called Holland Square, but its title was changed by request of the recipients. As according to the terms of the deed, business houses are not permitted to encroach upon this locality, it still remains a desirable down-town place of residence. These grounds once formed the northern portion of the Stuyvesant farm, which extended southward to 3rd Street, and from Third Avenue eastward to the river. On a spot within this farm, now identified by a plate at the corner of 11th Street and Third Avenue, there flourished for nearly two hundred years a pear tree which was brought from Holland by the original Peter Stuyvesant, and planted by him to preserve the memory of his name.

THE FRIENDS' MEETING HOUSE AND SEMINARY are at the left of Stuyvesant Square. The Quakers, who suffered much persecution at the hands of Dutch governors, as well as from Puritan authorities, could not firmly establish themselves in this city until the beginning of the eighteenth century, when they erected their first meeting-house near Maiden Lane. Since that time they have successively put up a number of buildings, but at present these just referred to, belonging to the Hicksite branch, and one other, belonging to the orthodox sect, are the only meeting-houses that remain standing. Through all the vicissitudes of the city's growth the Quaker element ever has been bold, peaceful, prudent, and practical, and our present prosperity owes much to their discreet activity.

Saint George's Church, (Episcopalian) at the 16th Street corner, is in its architectural style a transition from the Romanesque to the Gothic. Two spires of such beautiful proportions that they challenged general admiration, recently have been taken down because they were considered unsafe. Fortunately they are to be rebuilt. This church originally was one of three chapels belonging to Trinity Corporation, but it became a distinct charge in 1811. Its first edifice was erected in 1752, on ground near Beekman Street, called "Chapel Hill." The present structure was built in 1849. For many years this parish was presided over by the celebrated Dr. Stephen H. Tyng, whose remarkable insight and energy organized a work which is now ably continued and enlarged by the present rector, Dr. W. S. Rainsford. The presence of thirty women in the vested choir is an innovation and improvement in the service. The building at the rear is a sort of church club-house, where members have the advantages of reception and class rooms and a fine gymnasium.

Sixteenth Street extends westward from Saint George's to Irving Place, and Irving Place leads southward to East 14th Street.

A picturesque little theatre called the "Amberg,"—formerly Irving Hall,—at the corner of Irving Place and 15th Street, is appropriated to German plays.

THE ACADEMY OF MUSIC, at the 14th Street corner, was built in 1854 and rebuilt in 1866. Although the exterior of this edifice is very plain, the interior is renowned for its perfect appointments. Italian opera long found a home in this building, during which time its walls echoed to the world's most perfect voices. Great dramatic stars, among them Rachel, Ristori, Booth, Salvini, and Janauschek, also have appeared upon its stage. Until the erection of the Metropolitan Opera House the Academy was the popular place for balls and public meetings, but it is now entirely used for dramatic presentations.

TAMMANY HALL, which is situated east of the Academy in 14th Street, is headquarters for the Tammany Society, or Columbian Order, —an organization founded in 1789 for the purpose of perpetuating a true love of country. In order to propitiate the Indians the society adopted aboriginal forms and christened itself with the name of an Indian chieftain. At first a national society, based upon general principles of patriotism and benevolence, it became partisan when the administration proclaimed neutrality during the French Revolution. It is now the most thoroughly organized political body in the country, polling about half of the entire city vote. Every district has its committee, which is under the direction of a general committee of eleven hundred members, who are in turn controlled by a "Grand Sachem," or "boss." It was this order which inaugurated the perpetual commemoration of Washington's birthday. The first Tammany Hall, or "Wigwam," stood on the site now occupied by the *Sun* Building. The present edifice was built in 1867.

STEINWAY HALL, once made classical by the best concert music, but now converted into piano warerooms, was in the Steinway Building, at the west of the Academy in 14th Street.

UNION SQUARE.—A few steps eastward and an open park is reached, which affords a breathing space to the public in the very heart of the city. Business has so engrossed this locality that but very few of the old residences remain. A flag-stone in the sidewalk at the east side, upon the surface of which is cut, "Union Square, founded in 1832," identifies the former home of the person who was most active in securing the early improvements for this place, Mr. Samuel Ruggles.

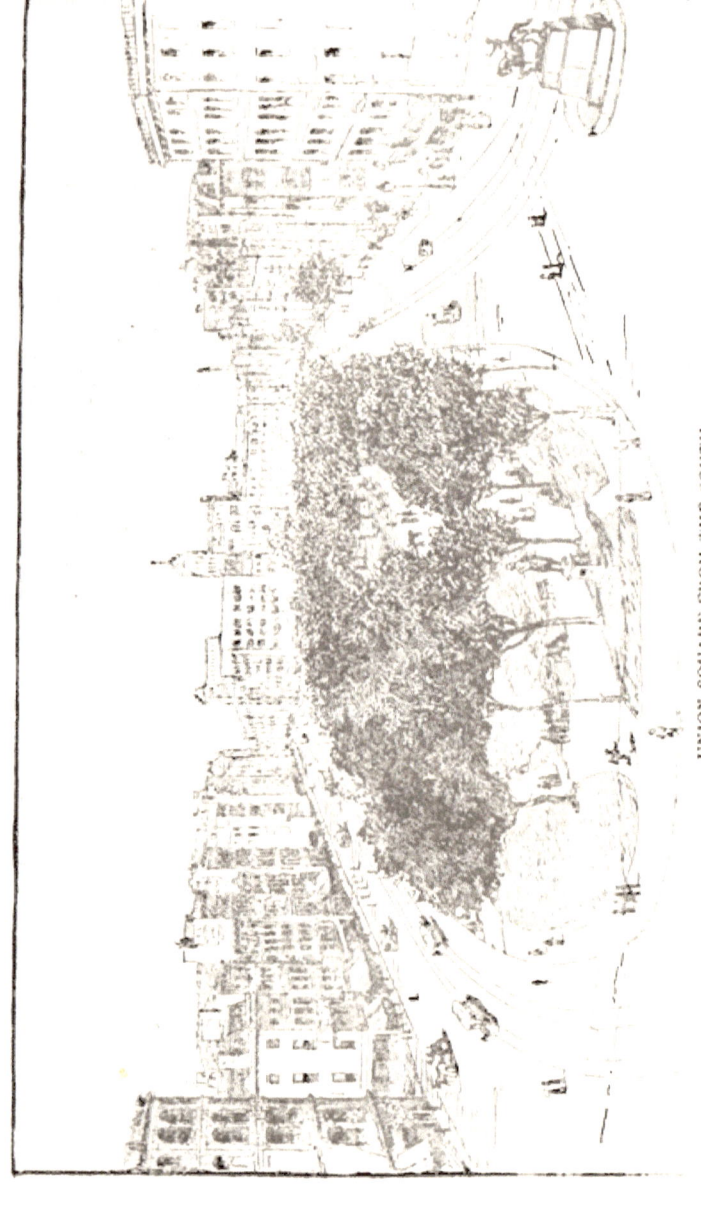

UNION SQUARE FROM THE SOUTH.

THE COLLEGE OF SOCIAL ECONOMICS, which occupies the southeastern corner of 16th Street and Union Square, represents a new departure in educational lines, its object being to found a School of Economics that shall be distinctly American, thus giving to students a broader basis upon which to form a judgment of new social conditions than is made possible by application of the doctrines of the Manchester School. A business college forms a part of the institution, and free lectures on themes of popular interest are delivered Wednesday evenings.

THE BRONZE EQUESTRIAN STATUE OF WASHINGTON, of heroic size, which stands near 14th Street, was the first public work of art ever set up out-of-doors in this city. It was erected in 1856 by enterprising merchants. H. K. Brown was the sculptor.

THE GREAT WAR MEETING OF 1861, called in response to Lincoln's appeal for troops "to sustain the Federal Government in the present crisis," was held under this fac-simile of the benign face of our first President.

The park contains about three and one-half acres of ground that are kept in excellent order. The fountain pond is filled with exotics similar to those already observed in other parks, and bordered with brilliant foliage plants. From the balcony of the cottage north of the fountain officials review the parades that frequently take place on the 17th Street Plaza, banners and a row of gas-jets making the place brilliant on special occasions. A drinking fountain stands at the western edge. The bronze statue of Lincoln, erected by popular subscription shortly after his assassination, and modeled by H. K. Brown, is at the southwestern corner. A statue of Lafayette, facing toward the south, was modelled by Bartholdi, and erected in 1876 by French residents in token of gratitude for the sympathy for France shown by America during the Franco-Prussian war.

Union Square Theatre faces the park at the 14th Street side. The pavement in front of this theatre is popularly known as the "Slave Market," from the fact that actors make this their lounging place while waiting for engagements.

WEST FOURTEENTH STREET, which well may be called "Vanity Fair," is the great shopping centre of New York, as the perpetual crowd, the bargain announcements in the shop windows, and the street venders of every description of goods, from choice roses to stove-blacking, will testify.

MACY'S, at the corner of 14th Street and

Sixth Avenue, represents a small world of traffic in itself. At first but an insignificant shop in an out-of-the-way quarter, it afterward succeeded in forcing trade to its own locality and became the nucleus of the present business of the street. Within this great mart may be found every variety of dry-goods and notions; also confectionery, drugs, books, magazines, stationery, toys, shoes; a fine restaurant, a glove department, a saddlery-hardware department, and a department of ceramics, bronzes, silverware, etc. In short, nearly everything, down to the simplest of household utensils, and all at moderate prices. Like Whitely of London, Macy has aimed to be an "universal provider," and it will be seen that he has practically succeeded.

It is a curious sight to watch the purchasers who often stand three and four deep around the counters. Women of wealth and simply-dressed country dames jostle each other in their efforts to secure the attention of the ever busy clerks. Children clap their hands at sight of a beneficent Santa Claus dispensing beautiful toys, or wail from the nervous fatigue of so much excitement, while cash girls in bright red aprons run hither and thither with their package baskets, endeavoring with all their might to expedite matters for the crowd that seems never to diminish and never to cease buying. It was Macy who originated prices in odd numbers, and also the Christmas window,—a moving panorama which annually proves so attractive that during the holiday season it becomes necessary to stretch a canvas across the stairway at the elevated-railway station in order to prevent spectators from using the stairs as a platform from which to view the windows.

THE SALVATION ARMY QUARTERS are in 14th Street, west of Sixth Avenue.

THE NEW YORK HOSPITAL, which now occupies a building in 15th Street, between Sixth and Fifth Avenues, was chartered by George the Third in 1771, and was the second organization of its kind in this city. The original edifice in Duane Street, was destroyed by fire before patients could be admitted, and having been rebuilt, was occupied by American and British soldiers until the close of the war; so that it was 1791 before the real work of the institution could begin. Since that time, however, the hospital has been almost unrivalled as a School of Medicine and Surgery. The present building, which is modern French Renaissance in design, was opened in 1887 with very perfect appointments, the upper story having been converted into a glass-roofed hall where patients may have the advantage of a sun bath. The first hospital on the Island, etablished by the Dutch near the old fort, was demolished by the British.

THE YOUNG WOMEN'S CHRISTIAN ASSOCIATION BUILDING, between Fifth Avenue and Union Square, was founded in 1870 for the purpose of assisting young women who are dependent on their own exertions. Classes are here instructed in sewing, book-keeping, etc.; and an employment bureau assists women to find positions. The system also includes a circulating library and reading-room, supplied with current periodicals; a gymnasium, a board directory, an exchange for woman's work, concerts, lectures, and Sunday Bible instruction. An addition, called the Margaret Louisa Home, which accommodates working women with lodging and board, recently has been erected in 16th Street. The building was the gift of Mrs. E. F. Shepard; the Association is supported by voluntary contributions.

TIFFANY'S.—The great building at the corner of 15th Street and Union Square is the far-famed jewelry store of Tiffany and Company, an establishment which stands alone in the world because it is so great of its kind. Of course, as changes constantly are taking place, a description of what is displayed at any one time only will serve to convey an idea of the general characteristics of this institution.

Upon the first floor there is a bewildering assortment of diamonds and other jewels, silverware, fans, etc. In the northwestern corner, devoted to Russian manufactures, a silver vase testifies to the remarkable degree of excellence arrived at by Russian artificers.

The second floor displays a varied and most interesting collection of artistic work. Among the marble and bronze statuary placed in a little room near the elevator, is Edward Thaxter's "First Dream of Love,"—a life-size marble figure which challenges criticism as to the conception,—for a maiden asleep in an upright position, her limbs bound with a net, her feet unsupported by the ground, and trailing through bushes, is a confusing thought. The work, however, is good, and the infant "Love," who whispers in the maiden's ear, is skilfully modelled. A much more effective piece of work by the same artist is the bust of "Meg Merrilies," which occupies a pedestal in the same room.

Specimens of agatized wood from Arizona and Dakota, in which startlingly beautiful mineral colors have been produced by the wash of waters containing quartz in large quantities, are next shown. Near these curiosities are antiques in wrought brass, armor, etc.; while everywhere are clocks that make the air musical with the chimes of Grace, Trinity, or Old World cathedrals.

Under a canopy in an apartment at the north side of the building, stands a time-stained statuette of Diana, which was found in a sarcophagus near Athens, and is supposed to be two thousand five hundred years old. This figure is rather sturdy for the modern ideal of beauty, but its pose is calm and dignified. A bas-relief of a woman's head and shoulders, in which the workmanship is so delicate and the elevation so slight as to suggest the possibility of a sketch in marble, occupies a place on the wall near by. William Cooper is the creator of this last mentioned thing of beauty.

The collection in this apartment also contains an electrotype copy of the Bryant Vase, manufactured by Tiffany, and exhibited by him at Philadelphia in 1876.

A group of Russian bronzes at the left of the elevator should not be overlooked, as the quality of the material, the detail of the work, and above all, the consummate skill with which spirited action is portrayed in every object, make this exhibit a special feature of the establishment.

On the floor above ceramics from all the great factories of the world are displayed.

CHAPTER V.

THE THIRD MORNING.

"MILTON'S VISIT TO GALILEO" is the subject of a painting by Professor Gatti, of Florence, which is exhibited in the art room of J. H. Johnston and Company's jewelry store, No. 17 Union Square. The poet, who is gazing at the stars through a telescope, and the astronomer, who stands near him surrounded by his family, form a most interesting group, especially so when it is understood that each face is said to be an authentic portrait. The light from a candle in the hands of the maid, the rays from a lamp which is burning on the table, and the moonlight seen through the archway from which astronomical observations are being taken, form three luminous centres in which the proportionate relationships are maintained with a fidelity which attests great skill on the part of the artist. Extreme delicacy of drawing also is displayed in a chart of the heavens which stands on the table.

This art room also contains several excellent

specimens of the French and Spanish schools, and American art is well represented. An admirable likeness of Thomas Paine, said to be the only portrait of that celebrated individual which was painted from life, is one of the most noticeable features of this collection.

AN OLD MAJOLICA INKSTAND.—Among the ceramics exhibited in this establishment is a curious old inkstand which bears the significant date of 1492. Extremely clumsy in form, it is agreeable to look upon because of its harmonious coloring. The inscription on the cartouche, "I. H. S.," with cross and nails, and the device of the Medici family,—the six pills, —on a shield in the lower division, testify to the correctness of the supposition that this relic was manufactured in the Caffagiolo factory near Florence, for use in a monastery, thus relegating the formation of the quaint structure to a time only twenty-six years later than the Heraldic Shield which was exhibited with the Castellani collection at Philadelphia, in 1876. The Cluny Museum in Paris, and the Museum at Sévres, possess other pieces of the same school.

FROM UNION SQUARE TO TWENTY-THIRD STREET, Broadway is occupied by large retail dry-goods houses, and carpet and jewelry establishments; as well as by florists, caterers, dealers in ceramics, etc., all of whom draw their patronage from among the wealthy class.

"CHOOSING THE BRIDE," by Makoffsky.— This elaborate painting, which is a companion piece to the "Russian Wedding Feast," is exhibited in Schumann's uptown jewelry store, at the corner of Broadway and 22d Street. The critical moment when a Russian prince selects his consort from a group of radiant beauties is the subject here portrayed. The dramatic action is not so fine in this as in the first-named picture, but the costumes and jewels of the noble damsels are quite as elaborate, and the scheme of color is harmonious and brilliant. An admission fee of twenty-five cents, which is appropriated to charity, is charged.

THE RESIDENCE BUILT FOR SAMUEL J. TILDEN is in Gramercy Park, two blocks east of Broadway, at Nos. 14 and 15 East 20th Street. The stone carvings on the exterior of this edifice are of great artistic excellence, the entire façade being enriched with divisional bands of beautifully sculptured foliage, and bas-relief figures cut in sunken disks, while the delicately chiselled heads of Shakespeare, Milton, Franklin, Goethe, and Dante, appear on a panel near the eastern entrance.

THE PLAYERS' CLUB HOUSE, at No. 16 East

20th Street, is a gift to actors from the founder and president of the club, Edwin Booth. The building contains the libraries of Mr. Booth and Lawrence Barrett, and also the play bills collected by Augustin Daly. A general rendezvous of players takes place in these apartments every Saturday night.

GRAMERCY PARK is open to residents in the immediate neighborhood only. Cyrus W. Field, David Dudley Field, John Bigelow, and other well-known persons, occupy houses in this attractive locality.

Lexington Avenue, which extends northward from Gramercy Park, contains the former home of Peter Cooper. The residence of the philanthropist was at No. 9.

THE COLLEGE OF THE CITY OF NEW YORK stands at the southeastern corner of Lexington Avenue and 23d Street. Each year nearly one thousand young men here receive tuition in a classical, scientific, or mechanical course. A post-graduate course in engineering occupies two additional years. The college contains a fine library, a cabinet of natural history, and apparatus for the use of the scientific department. The institution is maintained at an annual cost to the city of about one hundred and fifty-three thousand dollars.

Bellevue Hospital Medical College, and

Training School for Nurses are at the foot of East 26th Street. This hospital was founded in 1826, and is under the control of the city government; but the college, an independent institution, was not organized until 1861.

THE ASSOCIATED ARTISTS occupy premises at No. 115 West 23d Street. This is a stock-company of women, who are placing a commercial value on the talents of women, and who expect eventually to make of their organization a School of Design which shall be distinctly American. Embroidering and decorative drawing and designing for wall paper, tapestries, and fabrics, are taught to the pupils of this establishment, who become a part of the institution after a three years' course. To those persons who are investigating the progress of decorative art nothing can be more delightful than a few moments spent in examining the products of this fairy workshop. Silks, soft and fine as any woven in Oriental looms, and with colors so perfectly combined that artists frequently suppose the material to have been treated with the brush, delight the eye, while the patriotic sense is gratified with the knowledge that only American flora and fauna form the basis of the designs for these exquisite fabrics. Many color studies in textiles and tapestries are displayed, in which the workmanship seems little short of marvellous. A characteristic feature of the tapestry-work is the poetic thought woven in with the threads. At the present time deft fingers are producing a series of curtains that portray the heroines of Hawthorne's novels with such unmistakable originality of design that the artist, Dora Wheeler, is immediately recognized. Visitors are welcome at the showrooms of this establishment throughout the day.

THE NATIONAL ACADEMY OF DESIGN.—
The beautiful structure of artistically blended gray and white marble and blue stone, standing at the northwestern corner of Fourth Avenue and 23d Street is in part a copy of the Palace of the Doges in Venice, its architectural design being the Italian Gothic. The vestibule floor is of variegated marbles, and a massive marble stairway leads to the galleries above. Here every spring and autumn, an exhibition of new paintings takes place, and prizes are awarded. Other organizations sometimes rent these galleries for the display of their art work among them the American Water Color Society holds an annual exhibition during the month of January, which is extremely popular. Free art schools and lecture rooms, open to both sexes from October until

June of every year, occupy the first and second floors of the building.

The inception of the Academy, now the foremost art institution in the country, was due to Professor S. B. Morse, who was himself an artist of no mean ability. About the year 1815 he founded a society of artists of which he became president, and before which he

THE NATIONAL ACADEMY OF DESIGN.

delivered the first course of lectures on the fine arts ever given in this part of the world. Although this organization thrived, its existence was nomadic until 1863, when the present building was erected, and dedicated with imposing ceremonies.

The members of the institution consist of academicians (N.A.), and associates (A.N.A.), who acquire either rank of professional distinction by merit.

THE YOUNG MEN'S CHRISTIAN ASSOCIATION BUILDING is opposite the Academy, at the southwestern corner of 23d Street and Fourth Avenue. This edifice, which is French Renaissance in design, contains a reception and reading room; a concert hall, seating four thousand, a lecture room, library, gymnasium, and bowling-alley; besides parlors, class-rooms and baths. The building is open every day in the year, including holidays, and many opportunities for instruction and entertainment are afforded the members. The association has six branch organizations in different parts of the city.

CHAPTER VI.

THE THIRD AFTERNOON.

THE AMERICAN ART ASSOCIATION.—The beautiful galleries of this institution at No. 6 East 23d Street, usually are occupied with interesting collections of paintings. The association holds two exhibitions yearly, at which prizes valued at two thousand dollars are awarded for the best paintings, while gold medals worth one hundred dollars are bestowed for works of secondary merit.

MADISON SQUARE, which is bounded at the south and north by 23d and 26th streets, and at the east and west by Madison Avenue and the intersection of Broadway with Fifth Avenue, contains about six acres of ground, made beautiful with shade trees, flowers, and a fountain.

Until the year 1847 this part of the Island was rather unsightly, and previous to the time of its improvement, was occupied only by Corporal Thompson's little yellow tavern, and an old arsenal which was utilized as a house of refuge. At present this park is the centre of

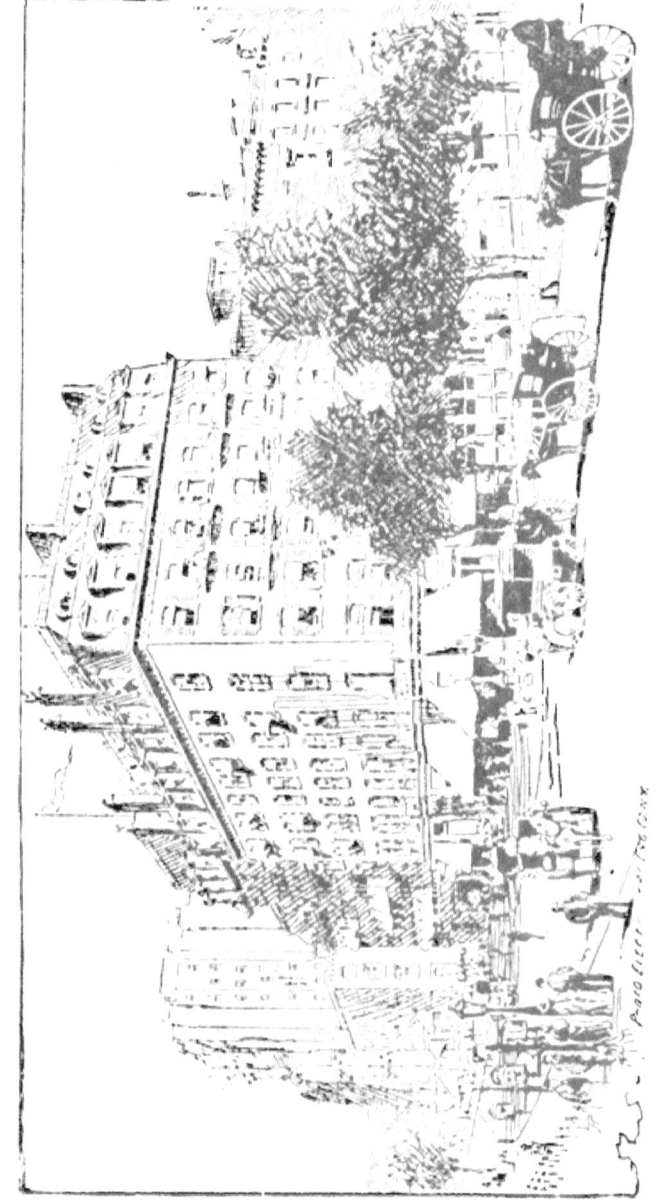

MADISON SQUARE AND FIFTH AVENUE, LOOKING NORTHWARD.

a world of fashion and amusement. The
Madison Avenue side is occupied by the Metropolitan Life Insurance Company Building,—
an example of the Italian Renaissance style of
architecture, very rich in its material and detail,—a Presbyterian church, and the building
which formerly belonged to the Jockey Club,
and later to the Union League, but is now the
home of the University Club. In this organization membership is restricted to men who
have graduated from some college, university,
or professional school, from the United States
Military Academy at West Point, or the United
States Naval Academy at Annapolis.

MADISON SQUARE GARDEN.—The most conspicuous building in this vicinity is situated
in Madison Avenue, between 26th and 27th
Streets. Its ornate style attracts immediate
attention. The architectural design, partly
Moorish, and partly Spanish Renaissance, is
novel to us, and the arrangement of electric
lights, fantastically grouped about the minaret
domes and the tower, until they terminate in a
brilliant crescent under the feet of the bronze
Diana at the apex, is an exceedingly pleasant
vision, suggesting unlimited delights for summer evenings in the garden on the roof. The
auditorium has a seating capacity of fifteen
thousand. Boxes and galleries surround its

walls, and tables as well as chairs, are placed on the main floor for the benefit of those who desire refreshment during the performances. Concerts, spectacular displays, horse, bench, and flower shows, that require commodious accommodations, usually form the attractions

MADISON SQUARE GARDEN.

at this place. The northern portion of the building contains a small theatre and a beautiful concert hall. An elevator carries visitors to the tower for twenty-five cents.

The old Madison Square Garden, which formerly occupied this site, had previously been known as Gilmore's Garden; earlier, it was

Barnum's Hippodrome, and for many years before that time it was a passenger station of the Harlem Railway.

Madison Avenue extends northward from this point to Harlem.

THE MONUMENT TO ADMIRAL FARRAGUT, which stands at the northwestern corner of Madison Square, is much admired. It was erected by the Farragut Memorial Association, and the statue was made by Augustus St. Gaudens.

THE WORTH MONUMENT, at the intersection of Broadway and Fifth Avenue, is the most prominent object in Madison Square. It is a granite obelisk, erected by the corporation of the city in memory of Major-General Worth; who first achieved distinction at Chippewa, under General Scott in 1841, and afterward participated in the war with Florida Indians,— 1840 to 1842,—and in the Mexican struggle of 1846 to 1848. The name of Anthony Street was changed to Worth Street in honor of this soldier.

THE STATUE OF WILLIAM H. SEWARD, by Randolph Rogers, which is placed at the southwestern corner of the park, represents that statesman in a sitting posture, surrounded by huge tomes. It was unveiled in 1876.

The white marble building at the north-

western corner of Fifth Avenue and 23d
Street, is the Fifth Avenue Hotel, which at
the time of its completion in 1859, caused the
residents of the city to wonder how so costly
an edifice could obtain sufficient patronage at
this then remote locality.

GOUPIL'S ART GALLERY, at the corner of
22d Street and Fifth Avenue, always contains
a choice assortment of paintings. The other
standard galleries are: Wunderlich's, No. 868
Broadway, Schaus's, No. 204 Fifth Avenue,
Reichard's, No. 226 Fifth Avenue, Avery's,
No. 368 Fifth Avenue, and Keppel's, No. 20
East 16th Street.

TWENTY-THIRD STREET.—West of Madison
Square, 23d Street for one or two blocks, is a
modified reproduction of 14th Street, although
it is somewhat less democratic in character.
The business building at the southeastern corner of 23d Street and Sixth Avenue was formerly Edwin Booth's elegant theatre, built
and made famous by Booth himself.

The Masonic Temple, which is headquarters
for the Masonic order throughout the State,
occupies the northeastern corner of the same
thoroughfares. This building was erected in
1867. For several blocks north and south from
this point Sixth Avenue vies in importance
with Broadway as a retail business street.

EDEN MUSÉE.—This attractive museum is situated on the northern side of 23d Street, between Sixth Avenue and Madison Square. The exhibition mainly consists of life-like wax figures of noted persons grouped in historical tableaux, and musical performances are given.

MADISON SQUARE THEATRE.—This is a beautiful little house, just west of Madison Square, in 24th Street. The decorations are exceedingly artistic. The drop-curtain is a marvel of embroidery, worked by the skilled hands of the Associated Artists. A novel feature of this house is its double stage, one part of which can be lifted and arranged while the performance is being conducted upon the other. The orchestra occupies a gallery above the stage.

NYMPHS AND SATYR, by William Bouguereau.—This great painting which is exhibited in the Hoffman House Café, in 24th Street, opposite the Madison Square Theatre, is considered by the eminent artist himself to be one of his most important works. The trees seem to balance in the wind, and the flesh tints are superb; the attitudes of the nymphs,—who pose in every variety of position as they play with a satyr whom they are endeavoring to force into the water,—are such wonderful studies in anatomical structure as to announce the master whose art almost conceals the evidence of art.

NARCISSUS, by Correggio, another of the choice paintings in this remarkable collection, delights the eye with its deep color-tones.

A PIECE OF GOBELIN TAPESTRY,—made for Napoleon the Third,—representing the port of Marseilles, will challenge extreme admiration for the delicacy of its tints and the perfection of its design.

A PIECE OF FLEMISH TAPESTRY, taken from Constantinople during the Russo-Turkish War, represents a scene at the wedding feast of Queen Hester.

Other fine paintings decorate the walls, and statues, placques, vases, rare plants, and curious old clocks, adorn this most palatial of bar-rooms. Ladies visit the café, even without the attendance of gentlemen, during any hour of the day.

THE HOFFMAN HOUSE.—Many beautiful examples of decorative art are displayed in this hotel. The gorgeous banquet hall suggests "Aladdin's cave," and the private dining rooms, modelled from French, Turkish, Moorish, and other foreign apartments, and filled with curiosities from the civilizations of the old world, are most interesting. A collection of fine paintings hangs on the walls of the parlors and corridors.

NORTH BROADWAY.—Several of the most popular theatres occupy prominent positions in Broadway between Madison Square and 34th Street. Among them may be mentioned Daly's, Palmer's (formerly Wallack's), The Fifth Avenue, Hermann's, etc. The Broadway Tabernacle, a Congregational church of which Dr. Taylor is the pastor, stands at the corner of 34th Street, where Broadway crosses Sixth Avenue. The bronze statue of William E. Dodge standing in the triangular space near by, was erected by the merchants of New York, in 1885. The Park Theatre is conspicuous at the left.

The Casino, a Moorish structure at the southeastern corner of Broadway and 39th Street, is devoted to the presentation of comic opera. The architectural design of this edifice is an adaptation of the Palace of the Alhambra in Spain, excellently carried out in detail. The interior contains a bewildering variety of arches, galleries, and foyers, so pleasing as frequently to divert attention from the stage. A lantern-lighted garden on the roof offers a delightful resort for summer evenings.

THE METROPOLITAN OPERA HOUSE.—The edifice occupying an entire block between 40th and 41st Streets, is an example of a very simple treatment of Italian Renaissance. The auditorium, which is enormous, contains one hundred and twenty-two boxes, each of which is connected with a salon in which refreshments may be served or visits received. Smaller rooms for concerts and lectures also are provided, and are constantly patronized. The building was opened in 1883, under the management of Henry Abbey. Since that time it has been principally devoted to splendid presentations of the German and Italian opera, although great balls and mass meetings are held here during the season.

THE WORKING-MEN'S SCHOOL.—This institution is situated east of Seventh Avenue (into which the car enters at 43d Street), at 109 East 54th Street. Educators and philanthropists from all parts of the world visit this place in order to study the methods that have been successfully conducted by the Society for Ethical Culture.

MUSIC HALL.—The close of the musical season of 1890–91 was made memorable by the opening of the edifice at the southeastern corner of Seventh Avenue and 57th Street, an event made possible through the munificence of Andrew Carnegie. This stately structure, a very good example of the Italian Renaissance style of architecture, will change the centre of musical life from the vicinity of Union Square to the Central Park region,—close to the spot at the corner of Seventh Avenue and 59th Street, where Theodore Thomas, in his summer garden concerts, may be said to have inaugurated his career as a musical conductor.

The building contains a series of halls adapted to every variety of musical assemblage. Main Hall has a seating capacity of about three thousand, and is very perfect in its ventilation and acoustic properties. Recital Hall, Chamber Music Hall, and Chapter Room, comprise the other apartments, all of which are provided with the requirements necessary for the purpose indicated by their names, and decorated with tasteful elegance.

The Broadway Line terminates at 59th Street and Seventh Avenue, where the Navarro Flats, called the "Madrid," "Cordova," "Lisbon," and "Granada," are situated. The cost of these sumptuous apartment houses was more than seven millions of dollars.

CHAPTER VII.

THE FOURTH MORNING.

FOURTH AND MADISON AVENUES.—The uptown portion of Fourth Avenue extends northward from Union Square to 32d Street.

ALL SOULS' UNITARIAN CHURCH, formerly presided over by the celebrated Dr. Bellows, stands at the southeastern corner of Fourth Avenue and 20th Street. The New York Flower Mission receives its supplies in the basement of this building.

THE AMERICAN SOCIETY FOR THE PREVENTION OF CRUELTY TO ANIMALS,—made effective by the herculean efforts of the late Henry Bergh,—formerly occupied the building at the 22d Street corner, but is now temporarily domiciled at No. 10 East 22d Street. The old Boston Post Road turned eastward at this point, passing along the outskirts of Rose Hill Farm, the home of General Gates.

THE LYCEUM THEATRE is directly north of the Academy of Design. This play-house is renowned for the moral character of its presentations. The Fourth Avenue Studio Building is at the corner of 25th Street. Besides this, and the one already mentioned in 10th Street, the other buildings devoted exclusively to artists are: "The Sherwood," in West 57th Street near Sixth Avenue, "The Rembrandt," near Seventh Avenue in West 57th Street, "The Holbein," 139 to 145 West 55th Street, Nos. 140 to 146, at the opposite side of the same street, and No. 106 West 55th Street. There are also a number of studios in the Young Men's Christian Association Building, and in the old Manhattan Club Building, at the corner of Fifth Avenue and 15th Street. To some of these studios visitors are admitted at any time, while a special reception day is appointed for others. The janitors usually can tell what studios are open.

MURRAY HILL rises at 32d Street, where the ground is tunnelled for the passage of the horse cars. Above the tunnel a series of openings surrounded with flowers, gives the street the appropriate name of Park Avenue. At the corner of 32d Street stands a building which was erected by the late A. T. Stewart for a working-women's home. The experiment proved a failure because of the stringent rules, and the structure was converted into a hotel called "The Park Avenue."

Considerable bric-à-brac from the Stewart Mansion now decorates the interior of this building.

THE CHURCH OF THE MESSIAH, of which the Rev. Robert Collyer is the pastor, is at the corner of Park Avenue and 34th Street. This rise of ground once formed the estate of Robert Murray, the "Quaker Merchant of the Revolution," and the father of Lindley Murray, the grammarian. The place was known as "Inclenberg," and became historic through the adroit diplomacy of Mrs. Murray, who, by her hospitality and grace, detained the British officers, Howe, Clinton, and Cornwallis; while Putnam and his column, guided by Aaron Burr, passed within half a mile of her house, at the time of their retreat to Harlem.

THE GRAND CENTRAL RAILWAY STATION, facing the tunnel at 42d Street, is the termini for the New York Central, the New York and New Haven, and the New York and Harlem railways, each of which has offices in the building, as well as passenger rooms. The space for trains is covered with a glass roof, having a single arch of a span of two hundred feet, and an altitude of one hundred and ten feet. The length of the building is six hundred and ninety-five feet. About one hundred and twenty-five trains arrive and depart daily, but confusion or crowding is almost unknown.

The site on which the station stands was once a cornfield belonging to the Murrays, into which the American soldiers plunged in their precipitate retreat from Kip's Bay. On a cross-road at about 43d Street, they were met by Washington, who is said to have been extremely severe in his condemnation of their panic.

MADISON AVENUE.—At 44th Street the horse-car tracks turn into Madison Avenue, whence they extend northward to Harlem.

ST. BARTHOLOMEW'S CHURCH, a good specimen of the Romanesque style of architecture, stands at the 44th Street corner.

THE MANHATTAN ATHLETIC CLUB HOUSE at the southeastern corner of 45th Street, is an attempt at the Romanesque, with Byzantine ornamentation.

THE RAILROAD BRANCH OF THE YOUNG MEN'S CHRISTIAN ASSOCIATION occupies the building at the northeastern corner of 45th Street. This edifice, which also is Romanesque in design, was a liberal contribution from Cornelius Vanderbilt.

COLUMBIA COLLEGE, which now occupies the buildings that cover the entire block between 49th and 50th Streets, was incorporated in 1754 as "Kings College," the necessary funds having been obtained from England. Recitations were first heard in the vestry-room of Trinity Church, but when a grant of land was obtained from the "Church Farm" (in Park Place, near the North River), college buildings were erected, and occupied by the students until the outbreak of the Revolution. After the war it became necessary to re-create the institution, as the library was found to be scattered and the buildings demolished. It was therefore re-incorporated in 1784 under its present name, and its management was vested in a self-perpetuating body of twenty-four trustees.

Among the many historical personages who acquired their scholastic abilities in this institution appear the names of Robert R. Livingston, Gouverneur Morris, John Jay, Alexander Hamilton, and De Witt Clinton.

The present buildings were mostly erected in 1857, when the Legislature granted twenty acres of ground to the college. Since that time its income chiefly has been derived from rentals of its real estate. In the near future the college probably will be removed to a site further uptown. The five collegiate departments are: the Schools of Art, Mines, Law, Political Science, and Medicine. The corps of instructors numbers about sixty, and the average attendance of students is about eighteen hundred. The college library, containing one hundred thousand volumes, is free to respectable strangers, as well as to students. Barnard College for women, at No. 343 Madison Avenue, is under the Columbia College instructors. The same regimen is required as for the male students. The Medical Department occupies a building in 60th Street, between Ninth and Tenth Avenues, which was a gift from William H. Vanderbilt. Connected with this is the Sloan Maternity Hospital, a gift from Mr. Vanderbilt's daughter, Mrs. Sloan. These magnificent donations, together with the Vanderbilt Free Clinic and Dispensary,—for which funds were contributed by Mr. Vanderbilt's four sons,—place the Columbia College of Physicians and Surgeons in the first rank for facilities as well as for instruction.

THE WOMAN'S HOSPITAL OF THE STATE OF NEW YORK is one block eastward, in Fourth Avenue. This organization, in which only women are treated, was founded by Dr. J. Marion Sims, and incorporated in 1857, by seven philanthropic ladies. The ground upon which the building stands formerly contained the remains of paupers and strangers, that several times had been transferred as the city grew northward. From here they were removed to Hart's Island, their present place of sepulchre.

A FLORENTINE PALACE in Madison Avenue at 50th Street, of brown sandstone, with an open court leading to three separate entrances, was built, but is not occupied, by Henry Villard. Climbing vines add greatly to the picturesque effect of this peculiar residence.

THE PALACE OF THE ARCHBISHOP, at No. 452, and the rectory, at No. 460, correspond architecturally with the cathedral, which, with them, forms a group of majestic proportions.

A Roman Catholic orphan asylum occupies the eastern side of the block between 51st and 52d Streets. The elegant Beekman Mansion, where the brave spy, Nathan Hale, was tried, condemned, and executed,—expressing in his last moments regret that he had but one life to lose for his country,—was in 51st Street, near the East River. Lenox Lyceum, a popular concert hall, is between 58th and 59th Streets. B'nai Jeshuron, a beautiful Jewish synagogue of Moorish design, is near 65th Street.

ALL SOULS' CHURCH (Episcopalian), of which the Rev. R. Heber Newton is pastor, is at the northeastern corner of 66th Street.

THE SEVENTH REGIMENT ARMORY.—At 66th Street it will be necessary to leave the cars and walk eastward for a short distance. The armory, in Fourth Avenue, between 66th and 67th Streets, is a massive edifice of red brick, with granite facings, constructed without regard to any particular style of architecture, but very perfect in its interior appointments. The main drill-room is very spacious, the dimensions being two hundred by three hundred feet. Visitors are admitted on application to the janitor.

Many interesting buildings are situated in this vicinity. Mt. Sinai Hospital is at the corner of 66th Street and Lexington Avenue, one block east of Fourth Avenue. The Chapin Home for the Aged and Infirm is in East 66th Street, at No. 151. The American Institute Hall,—in which industrial exhibitions are held every autumn,—is still further east, in Third Avenue at 63d Street. The Central Turnverein Building is in 67th Street, east of Third Avenue. A Moorish structure in 67th Street, west of Third Avenue, betrays the Jewish tabernacle. The Headquarters of the Fire Department are at Nos. 157 and 159 East 67th Street. Seventy-four companies are located in different parts of the city, and over one thousand alarm-boxes are placed at the street corners. The maintenance of the department, —in which about two thousand men are employed,—costs the city nearly two millions of dollars annually. A Deaf Mute Asylum is in Lexington Avenue, between 67th and 68th Streets. A Foundling Asylum (Roman Catholic) is in 68th Street, near Third Avenue. The Baptist Home for the Aged and Infirm is in 68th Street, near Fourth Avenue, and Hahnemann Hospital occupies a block in Fourth Avenue, between 67th and 68th Streets.

THE NORMAL COLLEGE FOR WOMEN, at the northeastern corner of 68th Street and Fourth Avenue, is under the control of the Board of Education, it being a part of the common school system. About one thousand and six hundred students annually are registered in this institution, seventy-five per cent of whom become teachers in the public schools. The college curriculum includes Latin, physics, chemistry, and natural science, German, French, drawing, and music; and the cost of maintenance is about one hundred thousand dollars a year. This edifice, which is in the secular Gothic style, with a lofty Victoria tower, is unsurpassed by any similar structure in the country.

THE UNION THEOLOGICAL SEMINARY OF THE PRESBYTERIAN CHURCH occupies the group of handsome buildings at the western side of Fourth Avenue, between 69th and 70th Streets.

This property is valued at two millions of dollars. The Presbyterian Hospital covers the block between 70th and 71st Streets, and Madison and Fourth Avenues. The Freundschaft Club House is in 72d Street, east of Fourth Avenue, and the Flemish mansion, built for Mr. Tiffany, but until recently the elegant home of Mr. Henry Villard, is in 72d Street, at the northwestern corner of Madison Avenue.

After inspecting the exterior of this unique, but palatial residence, the visitor will be pleased to begin the tour of the principal residence street of the city,—far-famed

FIFTH AVENUE.

THE LENOX LIBRARY BUILDING, which stands in Fifth Avenue, between 71st and 70th Streets, was erected by James Lenox, at a cost of over one million dollars, and endowed by him with a permanent fund of two hundred and fifty thousand dollars. An example of the French classical Renaissance style of architecture this imposing structure is made most pleasing to the eye because of the extreme purity of its design. A façade of ninety-two feet faces Fifth Avenue, which, with the wings that support it on either side, forms a court that is completed by a high stone wall with

THE LENOX LIBRARY.

massive iron gates. The material used in the construction of this building resembles light granite, but is in reality Lockport limestone.

The library, which occupies the wings, contains about thirty thousand volumes, including: Shakesperiana, Americana, many first editions of the Bible, a perfect copy of the "Mazarin Bible," (the first complete printed book known, supposed to be the product of Gutenberg and Faust, at Mainz, in 1450); a large folio Latin Bible printed by Koberger, at Nuremberg, 1477,—which is densely interlined in the handwriting of Melancthon,—some "block books," that represent the stage of printing before movable types superseded the Chinese fashion of cutting the page on a wooden block, and many rare books from the early presses of Europe, the United States, and Mexico. There is also a valuable collection of manuscripts, to which recently has been added a twelve-thousand-dollar treasure superbly illustrated by Giulio Clovio. The picture gallery, occupying the main portion of the second floor, contains many fine paintings, chiefly modern. Among them are several Wilkies, Verboeckhovens, Stuarts, Reynolds's, and Leslies; also two Turners and two Copleys; besides an Andrea del Sarto, a Delaroche, a Gainsborough, and a Horace

Vernet. Munkacsy's "Blind Milton Dictating
'Paradise Lost' to his Daughters,"—which was
considered to be the gem of the Paris Exposition in 1878,—is one of the most attractive
paintings in the gallery. The collection also
embraces a large number of portraits, including one of Bunyan,—which is believed to be an
original,—and five of Washington, three having been painted by Rembrandt Peale, one by
James Peale, and one full-length by Stuart.
This gallery recently has been further enriched by the late Mrs. Robert L. Stewart, who
bequeathed to it her valuable paintings.

The library is open every week-day, except
Monday, from 10 A.M. until 5 P.M. No admission fee is charged.

Between the Lenox Library Building and
59th Street many stately mansions with broad
porches and richly decorated vestibules, suggest a most inviting hospitality. This portion of Fifth Avenue, and the streets that lead
eastward from it, quite recently have become
a fashionable residence quarter.

The Progress Club, an organization of Hebrew gentlemen, occupies the handsome
building at the northeastern corner of 63d
Street. This edifice is Italian Renaissance in
design.

The approach to the park entrance in 59th

Street, called the plaza, is surrounded by three elaborately constructed hotels. The elegant residence of Mrs. E. B. Alexander is at No. 4 West 58th Street. The home of Cornelius Vanderbilt, at the northwestern corner of 57th Street, is a beautiful specimen of the modern French Renaissance style of architecture. The English Gothic house at the southwestern corner of the same street, is the residence of Ex-Secretary William C. Whitney. C. P. Huntington is erecting a handsome mansion opposite, at the southeastern corner. The elaborate edifice in the early Gothic style, at the corner of 55th Street, is the Presbyterian church over which Dr. John Hall presides. St. Luke's Hospital occupies the northwestern corner of 54th Street. The Gothic structure at the corner of 53d Street, is St. Thomas' Episcopal Church. The interior of this building, which is particularly pleasing both in color and in architectural design, contains paintings by John La Farge.

THE VANDERBILT RESIDENCES.—The remarkably beautiful home of W. K. Vanderbilt, at the northwestern corner of 52d Street, is a very fine example of French Renaissance (just emerging from the Gothic) of the time of François the First. The connected brown-stone houses between 52d and 51st Streets, are occupied by the widow of William H. Vanderbilt, and her daughter, Mrs. Sloan. Mrs. Vanderbilt possesses a very choice collection of paintings, and her gallery has been very freely opened to the public in the past; but the abuse of this privilege, having necessitated much more rigid rules, it is now quite difficult to obtain admission. The Roman Catholic Male Orphan Asylum is opposite. No. 634 is the residence of D. O. Mills.

THE CATHEDRAL OF ST. PATRICK.—Between 51st and 50th Streets stands a white marble edifice, which is the finest church building in the United States. Its elaborate architecture is of the decorated Gothic, or geometric style, similar to that of the cathedrals of Rheims, Cologne, and Amiens, on the continent, and the naves of York Minster, Exeter, and Westminster, in England. Its length is three hundred and six feet, its width is one hundred and twenty feet, and its towers are three hundred and thirty-five feet, and nine inches in height. The Fifth Avenue entrance is at present very imposing, but its effectiveness will be greatly enhanced by the statues of the twelve apostles that eventually are to be placed within the grand portal.

The same architectural style is preserved throughout the interior of the cathedral.

ST. PATRICK'S CATHEDRAL.

Massive columns of white marble, elaborately sculptured, support springing arches of exquisite proportions. The ceiling is groined with richly moulded ribs and foliage bosses. The high altar is of marble, inlaid with semi-precious stones, with the divine passion carved in bas-relief on its panels. The tabernacle over the altar is decorated with Roman mosaics, precious stones, and a door of fine gilt bronze. The throne of the cardinal, which is Gothic in design, is at the right of the sanctuary. Among the beautiful stained-glass windows there are thirty-seven memorials. Many paintings adorn the walls, the most admirable of which, by Costazzini, hangs over the altar of the Holy Family. When the Chapel of Our Lady, which is included in the design, is completed, the entire cost of construction will be about two million, and five hundred thousand dollars.

The cathedral was projected by Archbishop Hughes in 1850, and dedicated by Cardinal McCloskey in 1879. It is open every day in the week.

The home of the Democratic Club is at No. 617.

The church edifice at the corner of 48th Street, is one of three belonging to the Collegiate Dutch Reformed Society, next to Trinity, the oldest and wealthiest ecclesiastical corporation in the country. This organization, chartered by William the Third in 1696, vests the title and management of its large property in a legislative body, called the consistory, in which each of the three churches is represented. The one just mentioned, the third of the series, is a fine specimen of ornamental Gothic architecture in brown stone. The residence of Jay Gould is at No. 579. The rooms of the American Yacht Club are in No. 574. No. 562 is the residence of J. W. Harper, Jr. The Windsor Hotel is opposite, between 46th and 47th streets. The Church of the Heavenly Rest (Episcopalian) is just above 45th Street. The residence of Chauncey M. Depew is around the corner, at No. 22 East 45th Street.

THE CHURCH OF THE DIVINE PATERNITY (Universalist), long known as Dr. Chapin's church, is at the southwestern corner of 45th Street. The interior decoration of this edifice is quite a departure from orthodox ecclesiastical styles. Musical services are held here Sunday evenings that offer a rare treat to visitors. Rev. Charles Eaton is the present pastor.

TEMPLE EMANUEL.—The attractive edifice with minaret towers, at the northeastern corner of 43d Street, is the finest specimen of Saracenic architecture in the city. The interior also is very elaborate, being profusely decorated with rich oriental colors. Rabbi Gottheil, who preaches in this synagogue, is popular with both Jew and Gentile.

THE CENTURY CLUB HOUSE, at No. 7 West 43d Street, is occupied by a society of the most influential literary, artistic, and professional celebrities. This association, founded in 1847, has but recently erected its present home, the ornate style of which represents the school of Italian Renaissance.

THE RESERVOIR.—The distributing reservoir of the Croton water-works, between 42d and 41st Streets, is one hundred and fifteen feet above tide-water, and has a capacity of twenty millions of gallons. Its sombre stone walls covered with vines, are rather picturesque than otherwise.

BRYANT PARK.—At the rear of the reservoir is another restful shady spot in the midst of the city's busy life. This plot of ground was covered in 1853, by the Crystal Palace, a building constructed of iron and glass, and erected for the purposes of an international exhibition. As a novelty it created great enthusiasm, and the display of sculpture and painting gave a special impetus to the patronage and culture of the fine arts. An attempt was made to maintain a perpetual art exhibition in the palace, but the worthy effort failed. The "House of Glass" was also the scene of a magnificent ovation to Cyrus W. Field, when, in 1858, the Atlantic cable had abolished the ocean as a barrier of intercourse. Shortly after this memorable event the beautiful building, with its glittering dome and lofty galleries, was destroyed by fire.

A colossal bronze bust of Washington Irving, which stands near the 40th Street entrance to the park, was executed by Beer, a European sculptor, and presented to the city by a private citizen, in 1866.

The Republican Club occupies commodious quarters at No. 450 Fifth Avenue.

THE UNION LEAGUE CLUB HOUSE.—The elaborate building of red brick and brown stone, at the northeastern corner of 39th Street, is Italian Renaissance in design, and occupies a site which displays its architectural features to very fine advantage. The interior decorations are extremely tasteful, and the arrangement of the halls, galleries, and various rooms is well suited to the requirements of cultured gentlemen. The library contains over three thousand volumes, besides rare collections of engravings and etchings. A magnificent fresco by La Farge adorns the ceiling of the dining-room. Landscape paintings, and portraits that are owned by the club, hang on the walls of the different apartments, but the galleries are reserved for monthly exhibitions of loan paintings. To these, ladies are admitted if provided with cards from members. The annual reception given by this club, is always one of the most brilliant of the New York season.

The Union League, really the child of the United States Sanitary Commission, was organized in 1863, as a league of men of "absolute and unqualified loyalty to the United States," who were unwavering in their efforts to suppress the Rebellion. The club is still the stronghold of the Republican party, but since the war it has been more social than political in its character.

The home of Austin Corbin is at No. 425. The rooms of the St. Nicholas Club are at No. 415. This society is composed exclusively of gentlemen of the Knickerbocker stock, the families of whom resided in New York State prior to 1785. The Brick Church (Presbyterian) is at the 37th Street corner. A former edifice belonging to this society once was a conspicuous feature of City Hall Park. No. 400 is the home of Robert G. Ingersoll. Pierre

Lorillard lives near by, at No. 389. One of the oldest and most fashionable of clubs, the New York, occupies the Queen Anne mansion at the 35th Street corner.

THE STEWART MANSION.—The former residence of the late A. T. Stewart, at the northwestern corner of 34th Street, was built about 1866, at a cost of two millions of dollars. It is constructed of pure white marble, and architecturally is a good exemplification of the classical Italian Renaissance. The rare paintings and statuary that Mr. Stewart collected, have been scattered in many directions, and the house having been unoccupied for several years has had the appearance of a stately mausoleum. It is now the home of the Manhattan Club,—an organization intended to advance democratic principles, and promote social intercourse.

The residence of William Astor is opposite the Manhattan Club House, at No. 350 Fifth Avenue. A former residence of the Astors recently has been replaced by the hotel at the 33d Street corner. The Knickerbocker Club House is at the northeastern corner of 32d Street. The members of this organization belong to exclusive social circles. Several coaching and polo teams form a part of the club institution. A new and elaborate hotel at the southwestern corner of 30th Street, is called the Holland House. Holland Church, the second of the Collegiate Dutch Reformed Society series, stands at the 29th Street corner. It is built of Vermont marble, in the Romanesque style of architecture, and in front of it is placed the "silver-toned bell," to which reference has been made. A silver baptismal basin, —procured in 1694, and engraved with a sentence composed by Dominie Selyns,—is another relic of the past, still in use in the Dutch Reformed Church recently erected at the corner of Second Avenue and 7th Street.

THE LITTLE CHURCH AROUND THE CORNER.—Just east from Fifth Avenue, in 29th Street, stands the Church of the Transfiguration, made famous because an actor was permitted burial rites at its altar. The Reform Club (Democratic), organized for the purpose of promoting ballot and tariff reform, has its home at the northeastern corner of 27th Street. The Hotel Brunswick is between 27th and 26th Streets, and Delmonico's is opposite, at the 26th Street corner. The historical house formerly the home of Professor S. B. Morse, is at No. 5 West 22d Street. The Union Club House, at the northwestern corner of 21st Street, is the home of a non-political institution ranking very high socially. The Lotos Club, which occupies the house at the northeastern corner of the same street, is composed of artists, actors, literary and professional men. This organization gives a series of receptions to ladies every year, when artist members exhibit their new paintings. No. 109 was the home of the late August Belmont, who possessed one of the finest collections of paintings in the country. Chickering Hall, at the 18th Street corner, is used for concerts, lectures, etc. The Society for Ethical Culture meets in this building every Sunday morning to listen to the eloquent discourses of Felix Adler. Mrs. Marshall O. Roberts lives at No. 107. Edwards Pierrepont resided at No. 103, and the home of Vice-President Levi P. Morton is at No. 85. The First Presbyterian Church is at the corner of 11th Street, and the Church of the Ascension is at the 10th Street corner.

THE ASCENSION OF CHRIST, by John La Farge.—This great painting, which occupies an area forty feet square, above the altar in the last mentioned church edifice, is considered to be, by many good critics, the most important work of its kind yet produced in the United States It is crowded with a multitude of life-size figures, ranged in ascending vaults on either side of the central Christ. The painting is very powerful both in color and sentiment, and may be viewed any afternoon, as the church is open daily at that time.

General Daniel E. Sickles lives at No. 31, and John Taylor Johnston at No. 8, after which residence Fifth Avenue emerges into

WASHINGTON SQUARE.—This inviting park occupies about nine acres of ground. In the early New York days it was a potter's field, surrounded by wretched shanties, and called Union Place. When in 1832, the city converted it into the Washington Parade Ground, and expended large sums of money for its improvement, fashionable residents were attracted to the locality, who gave to it the aristocratic features that have characterized it to the present time.

Washington Square has been the scene of several brilliant pageants, one of the most elaborate of which occurred November 1830, as a public demonstration of the sympathetic joy which America felt for the French people, who had dethroned their faithless and tyrannical monarch, Charles the Tenth. This celebration was participated in by members of every profession, officers of the army and navy, and a vast number of persons who represented the trades. Several individuals were present who had borne an active part in our own Revolution; among them were Ex-President Monroe (who died soon afterward), and two persons who had hoisted the American flag at the Battery after the departure of the British troops in 1783.

In 1889, during the centennial celebration of Washington's inauguration, the Square was one of the prominent places of interest in the city, the military and civic parade both passing through it. A wooden arch, erected for this occasion at the Fifth Avenue entrance, has been reconstructed in stone, as a memorial of the event. The corner-stone of this arch was laid May 1890, the Bible used during the ceremony having been the one on which Washington took the oath of office as first President of the United States.

A music-pavilion, a fountain, and a statue of Garibaldi, are placed in this park; the latter ornament, which was a gift to the city from Italian residents, is the work of Giovanni Turini.

An unsuccessful attempt has been made to secure ground in the Square for an entrance to the Hudson River tunnel, which probably will come to the surface in an adjacent street. This herculean enterprise is expected shortly to be complete. Two other equally great attempts to connect our Island with the shores east and west of us are being made, work having been egun on both. One project is to tunnel the East River from Long Island to our city, and the other is to bridge the Hudson River in order to make New York, instead of the towns on the New Jersey side, the termini of western railroads.

THE JUDSON MEMORIAL at Washington Square South.—A shining cross, at a height of one hundred and sixty-five feet, attracts attention every evening to a new and peculiar religious institution, which has just erected a series of buildings including, a church, apartment house, kindergarten, gymnasium, children's nursery, and young men's club. These together form a monument to the memory of Adoniram Judson, the first American foreign missionary. The incredible hardships and practical Christianity of this hero suggested a tribute that should be in keeping with his useful life. The church, which is free and within easy access of the poorer classes, and the institutions connected with it, are to be supported by the receipts of the apartment house. Rev. Edward Judson, a son of the missionary, is the present pastor of the church. It was he who projected the work, and secured by subscription, the funds necessary to materealize the project. The cost of construction, four hundred thousand dollars, was covered by the contributions of wealthy individuals from all parts of the country.

THE UNIVERSITY OF THE CITY OF NEW YORK.—The Gothic structure with four octangular towers, which stands at the eastern side

of Washington Square, was erected in 1835, the University having been established in 1831, by public-spirited merchants and professional men. Professor Samuel F. B. Morse, who was one of the first professors of this institution, invented the recording telegraph in a room within this building; and in another apartment near by, Professor John W. Draper first applied photography to the reproduction of the human countenance. Portraits of the chancellors, and of many distinguished members of the council and faculties, are on the walls of the council-room. Henry M. MacCracken, D.D., LL.D., is the present Chancellor.

The departments consist of the Schools of Art, Science, Medicine, and Law, the latter recently having been opened to women. There is a graduate and an undergraduate division, the latter having been successfully carried on since 1832, the former only since 1886.

Another building belonging to this corporation, is in 26th Street, near the East River. It was erected in 1879, and is appropriated to the Department of Medicine. Much of the instruction is given to students in Bellevue Hospital, which is close by.

At No. 9 University Place,—a street extending northward from the University to Union Square,—the New York College for the Training of Teachers instructs students who already have acquired the elements of a secondary education, the degree conferred being that of Bachelor of Pedagogy. The departments include the history, philosophy, and principles of education; the science and art of teaching psychology, and manual training. The college also provides, by an extension system, free classes for teachers, mothers, and children, and a free lecture-course for the public.

CHAPTER VIII.

THE FOURTH AFTERNOON.—THE DRIVE.

"THE CIRCLE," at Eighth Avenue and 59th Street, is the point at which Broadway terminates and the Boulevard begins.

THE TWELFTH REGIMENT ARMORY is situated at the corner of 62d Street and Ninth Avenue, and a similar structure, belonging to the Twenty-second Regiment, stands in the Boulevard, at 67th Street.

THE DAKOTA FLATS occupy the corner of Eighth Avenue and 72d Street.

THE SOMERINDYKE HOUSE, which once stood in Ninth Avenue, near 75th Street, was the home of royalty during its exile. Here Louis Philippe and his brothers, the Duc de Montpensier and the Comte de Beaujolais, taught school for their living; and here they were visited by Queen Victoria's father, the Duke of Kent.

THE APTHORPE MANSION, another residence of historic interest, was where Washington remained during the evacuation of New York, only retiring to Washington Heights with his

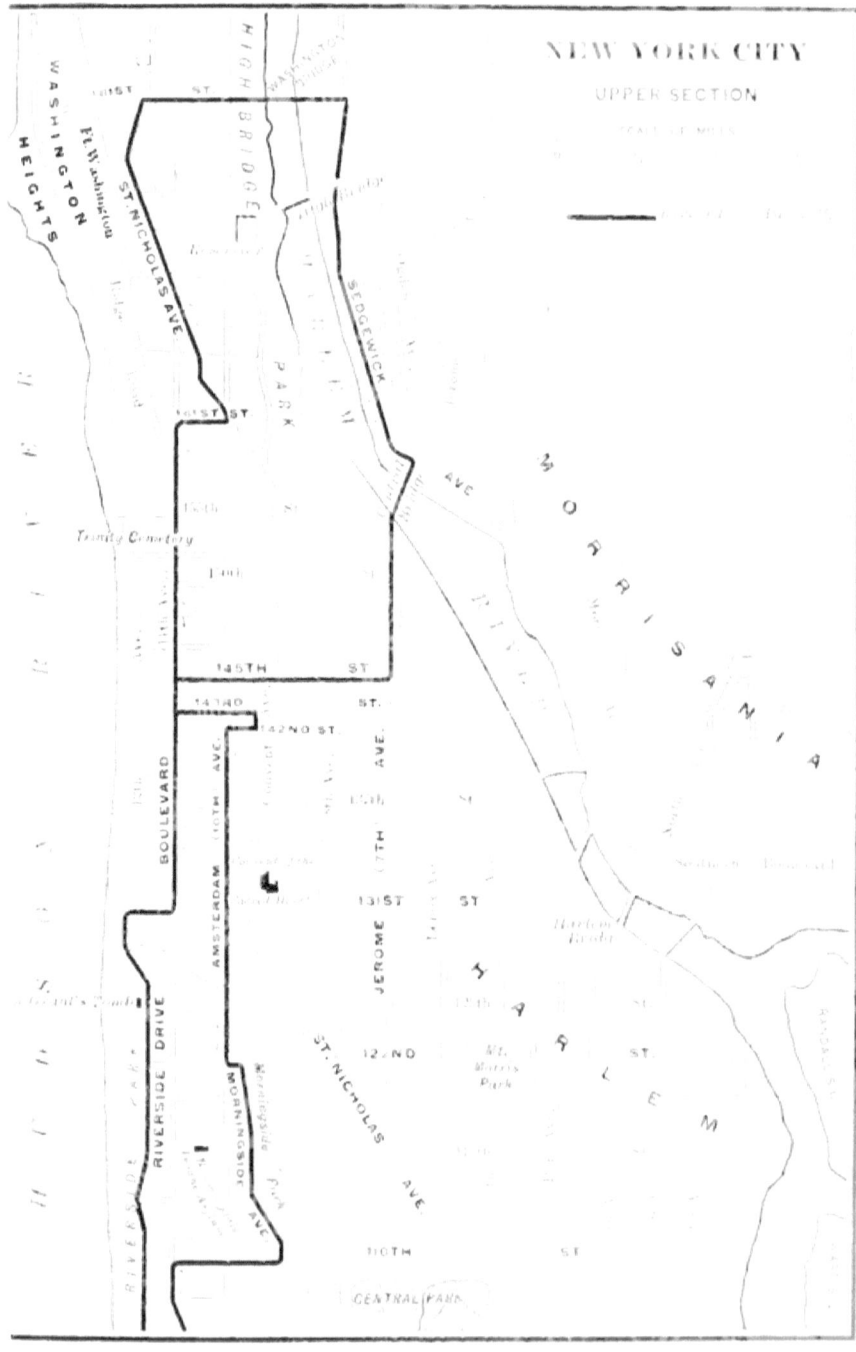

staff, one hour before the British officers took possession of the premises. This house stood at the corner of Ninth Avenue and 91st Street, and only recently has been demolished.

MORNINGSIDE PARK, lately appropriated for its present purpose, is now being improved by the park commissioners. A retaining wall rests on the western ledge, which forms the roadway called Morningside Avenue. Hanging terraces and a terrace walk greatly enhance the beauty of these grounds. The East River, the suburban region of Long Island, and the wooded hills beyond, are visible from that portion of the park which soon is to be converted into a mall, and embellished with shade trees. At 111th Street, where now stands the Leake and Watts Orphan Asylum, an elaborate and costly Episcopal cathedral is to be erected.

THE BLOOMINGDALE INSANE ASYLUM,—a department of the New York Hospital,—is in Tenth Avenue, between 114th and 120th Streets. This institution received its title from one of the many villages that were situated on the northern part of the Island before the city absorbed them all. The names of some of these little towns,—Manhattanville, Carmansville, and Harlem,—still remain to designate their old localities.

THE SHELTERING ARMS, at Tenth Avenue

and 129th Street, takes charge of homeless children for whom no provision is made in other institutions.

THE CONVENT OF THE SACRED HEART is situated in beautiful grounds above 130th Street and east of Tenth Avenue.

THE HEBREW ORPHAN ASYLUM is at 136th Street.

THE GRANGE, the former home of Alexander Hamilton, still stands in Convent Avenue, between 142d and 143d Streets. The house, which was named from Hamilton's ancestral home in Scotland, is well preserved, as is also the grove of thirteen trees that the proprietor set out as symbols of the thirteen original States. This planting was done with much pomp and ceremony in 1802, after a banquet given for the occasion, and with the speech-making, and solemnity of prayer, customary to the olden-time festivities.

Each tree is named for a State, and what is most peculiar, each tree has kept pace in its growth with the State which it represents. New York is the most majestic of the group, Pennsylvania is the next, and Rhode Island is a mere sapling as compared with the larger trees. The "crooked tree," South Carolina, at one time turned abruptly out of the grove, and then just as abruptly returned and grew

THE HAMILTON TREES.

straight   The State for which it was named,—the first to secede from the Union,—has been one of the most thrifty and flourishing since the restoration of peace.

"The Grange" was the residence of the statesman, at the time of his duel with Aaron Burr in Weehawken.

TRINITY CEMETERY.—The burial-ground for Trinity Church parishioners, since suburban interments were demanded, has been on either side of the Boulevard, above 153d Street. A wooden bridge over the roadway connects the eastern with the western portion. The Astor and the Audubon vaults are in this cemetery, also the vault of Madame Jumel.

The death of Colonel Thomas Knowlton is said to have occurred in this vicinity, in 1776, when, having been sent by Washington, (who was in the Morris House at 161st Street), to learn the position of the enemy, he met the advance guard and fell in the battle which followed.

To the right is "Breakneck Hill," so named by Thomas Jones,—the "fighting Quaker" of Lafayette's army,—who had helped to drive the British down its declivity.

The former home of Audubon, the great ornithologist, was directly north of Trinity Cemetery. Handsome residences are now attached to the original mansion, but the grounds are not divided by fences, and the place is very properly named Audubon Park.

THE MORRIS HOUSE.—This is one of the very few colonial residences extant. It is frame, painted white, and with the traditional pillars of its time adding dignity to its ripe old age. Overlooking the city and the quiet waters of the Harlem, it stands on a bluff at the corner of St. Nicholas Avenue and 161st Street.

THE ROGER MORRIS MANSION.

At first the property of Colonel Roger Morris, whose wife in her maiden days had been Washington's sweetheart, it afterward became the home of Madame Jumel, who was married to Aaron Burr in its drawing-room after the downfall of that distinguished individual. The most interesting memoirs connected with the history of this mansion are of course the events that occurred during the time when Washington made it his headquarters, while Howe occupied the Apthorpe residence, three and a half miles distant.

WASHINGTON BRIDGE was opened for travel in 1889. This magnificent structure, in which sections of steel are combined and keyed into the central arches instead of stone, is two thousand and four hundred feet in length, eighty feet in width, and one hundred and thirty-five feet in height. Its cost of construction was about two million, and seven hundred thousand dollars. From the bridge a beautiful view of the valley of the Harlem is obtained. Elegant residences and terraced grounds border the shores of the river, which is but a tidal channel connected with the Hudson by Spuyten Duyvil Creek, at the north of Manhattan Island. Through this section of the country legends innumerable abound, many of them having been immortalized by Irving. The queer name of the little creek recalls one of these, when Antony Corlear, on a stormy night, attempted to swim through the water from the island to the mainland, declaring that he would cross the current "in spyt den Duyvil" (in spite of the devil.) Improvements are eventually to be made at this point, in order to connect the East River with the Hudson by a ship-canal.

HIGH BRIDGE, which crosses the Harlem a little further south, supports an aqueduct for

HIGH BRIDGE.

the waters of the Croton River. This stone structure is built with thirteen arches that rest on solid granite piers. The length of the bridge is one thousand four hundred and sixty feet, and the crown of the highest arch is one hundred and sixteen feet above the river's surface. Pedestrians only can cross the bridge.

McCOMB'S DAM, or CENTRAL BRIDGE, is located near the plain where the last general

tion of turfmen were accustomed to speed their horses.

RIVERSIDE PARK consists mainly of a three-mile drive following the brow of the Hudson River bluff, from the meadows at 127th Street, formerly known as "Matje Davits' Fly," to 72d Street. Elegant residences adorn the eastern side of Riverside Avenue, and a good deal already has been done to beautify the park. At the right of the drive, where the ground slopes gently to the water's edge, grassplots and groves of shade-trees afford pleasant opportunities for a ramble. A massive retaining-wall supports the bank, whereon thousands of chattering birds build their nests, undismayed by the screaming locomotives that fly past them, bearing trains of cars over the New York Central Road. But the glory of this pleasure-ground consists in its extended vista of the Hudson. At the west repose in grandeur the Palisades,—a massive perpendicular wall of rock extending far toward the north;—at the north the wooded shores of the promontory, Fort Washington; at the south the towns of New Jersey; and in all of these directions the majestic river, with its sailing crafts and steamers, its endless combinations of light and shade, and its ever-changing hues of color.

CLAREMONT.—At the beginning of Riverside Drive, a restaurant now stands on the height which once was crowned by a stately private residence known as Claremont, and occupied successively by Lord Churchill, Viscount Courtenay, (afterward Earl of Devon), and Joseph Bonaparte, known as Comte de Survilliers.

THE TOMB OF GENERAL GRANT.—In the midst of this daily pageant of Nature, lie the remains of the great commander, General Ulysses S. Grant. After impressive ceremonies, and amidst a vast concourse of people, the body of this hero was laid to rest, August 8th, 1885, in the unpretentious vault which is placed at the east of the drive, in that portion of the park called Claremont Heights. A stately monumental structure soon is to be completed, which will add a dignity to this spot in keeping with its national and historical interest.

THE STATUE OF WASHINGTON, a copy of Houdon's work,—the one ornament of the kind yet placed in the park,—was a gift from the children of the public schools.

The residence of the late General Sherman was in West 73d Street, at No. 67.

CHAPTER IX.

THE FIFTH MORNING.

CENTRAL PARK, now the pride of the city, was a region of rock and swamp, but a comparatively short time ago, over which roamed at pleasure, the pigs, goats, and chickens, that belonged to the "squatters," whose shanties

OLD SQUATTER SETTLEMENT ON THE CENTRAL PARK SITE.

were perched on the hillsides, or clustered in the hollows.

The establishment of the park, which was effected in 1855, was greatly due to the untiring efforts of the Honorable De Witt C. Littlejohn, then speaker at Albany, now living in Oswego. This gentleman says, when the park is mentioned: "Yes, I fought hard for it, and thought the day we passed the bill the brightest in my life; but as I pass through it now, the trees that I planted thirty-five years ago do not know me, nor do the thousands of people who jostle me aside as they throng the beautiful roadways, heed me."

The value of the land appropriated to this purpose was estimated by the commissioners to be about five million, and two hundred thousand dollars; this amount to be paid partly by assessments on adjoining property benefited, and partly by the creation of a city-stock, called "The Central Park Fund," for the payment of which stock, the lands of the park should be pledged.

The cost of improving the grounds was provided for in the year 1857, by placing the management and control of the property under a Board of Commissioners, and requiring the corporation to create a public stock to be denominated "The Central Park Improvement Fund," in such sums as should be required by the commissioners,—the interest on the stock to be paid by a general tax, which was not to exceed one hundred thousand dollars annually.

The park, which now comprises about nine hundred acres, is situated very nearly in the geographical centre of the Island, and is in all respects well adapted to the recreative wants of both the rich and the poor. Pedestrians roam at pleasure over thirty miles of walks, —some fashionable and much frequented, others retired and quiet. Riders on horseback join the throng on the carriage roads, or confine their peregrinations to bridle-paths, on which no vehicle will be admitted. For carriages there are over nine miles of broad, well-made roadway, affording in its course a view of nearly every object of interest, but nowhere crossing on the same level, a footpath of importance, or any portion of the bridle-road.

In the improvement of the grounds the directions of the Board of Commissioners found expression through their executive officer, Mr. Frederic Law Olmsted, who made the designs, on which the arrangements were based, thus transforming the barren waste into a field of natural and artistic beauty, that rivals any similar pleasure-ground in the world. Incessant vigilance now maintains the park in perfect order, while the addition of trees, shrubs, and vines, continually increases the picturesque effect, and justifies the following of the wise counsel of the Laird of Dumbiedikes, whom

Mrs. Lamb quotes: "When ye hae naething else to do ye may aye be sticking in a tree; it will be growing when ye are sleeping."

THE MAIN ENTRANCE to the park is at the corner of Fifth Avenue and 59th Street.

THE ZOÖLOGICAL GARDEN. In and about the old arsenal, a castellated gray brick building, situated at the 64th Street and Fifth Avenue entrance, is located the menagerie, or by many now called the Zoölogical Garden.

During the summer months, the collection of birds and animals is small as compared with it when augmented by the travelling shows, that go into winter quarters here. The Monkey House, a building filled with tropical specimens of the monkey race, usually is the most attractive feature of the menagerie to the children. Here, of late, Mr. Garner, with the assistance of a phonograph, has pursued his scientific investigations concerning the speech of lower animals. In the meteorological observatory, also located in the arsenal, the self-recording instruments may be inspected.

THE STATUES OF THOMAS MOORE AND ALEXANDER VON HUMBOLDT are on the banks of the pond, not far from the main entrance. The former was modelled by Dennis B. Sheehan, and given to the city by the Moore

Memorial Committee; the latter was modelled by Gustave Blaeser, and presented to the city by German residents, on the one hundredth anniversary of the birth of the distinguished *savant*, September 14th, 1869. At the unveiling of this statue, Professor Louis Agassiz made a memorable address.

THE CHILDREN'S SHELTER, with a dairy, and an abundance of benches, seats, tables, and swings, is passed on the way to

THE MALL.—This prominent feature of the park is reached from the Zoölogical Garden by passing under the marble archway, a structure noted for the beauty of its architectural design. The mall itself is a broad promenade, one-third of a mile in length, ornamented on either side by rows of stately American elms, and terminating at the north in a richly decorated water-terrace and fountain.

The two exceedingly fine pieces of statuary, —Shakespeare, and the "Indian Hunter,"— that stand on the vestibule lawn at the southern approach to the mall, were executed by J. Q. A. Ward. A bronze casting of "Eagles and Goat," by Fratin, stands a little to the east. The other pieces, placed at either side of the promenade, are; Sir Walter Scott,—a copy of the original statue in Edinburgh,—by John Steele, Robert Burns, by the same artist, Fitz-Greene

ESPLANADE, FOUNTAIN, AND TERRACE IN CENTRAL PARK.

Halleck, by Wilson MacDonald, and a bust of Beethoven on a granite pedestal near the music stand. Concerts, that are listened to by vast numbers of people, are here provided for Saturday afternoons in the summer.

THE TERRACE AND ESPLANADE, that border the lake at the north of the mall, form the principal architectural feature of the park. Three stairways lead to the esplanade, the central one being under the road, and terminating in an arched hall decorated with tiles. The railing and stairways are constructed of light brown sandstone, with panels elaborately sculptured in great variety of intricate design. Especially rich, in pattern and execution, are the carvings of birds and animals, flowers and fruit, with which the noble ramps of the side stairways are decorated.

BETHESDA FOUNTAIN.—Hovering above the upper basin, with wings outstretched, as if just alighting on the massive rock at her feet, the figure of an angel appears to be in the act of blessing the waters of the fountain, which stands in the esplanade between the terrace and the lake. Four smaller figures, emblematic of the blessings of temperance, purity, health, and peace, support the upper basin, and are slightly veiled by the water which falls from above into the ample pond at their feet.

This work of art was designed and executed by Miss Emma Stebbins, of New York.

THE LAKE, a handsome, irregular pond, containing nearly twenty acres of water, is seen to the best advantage from the terrace. In the summer time gondolas, and pleasure boats of every description, sail its waters, while the winter months bring to it the gaiety which skating occasions. For a row about the lake the fare is ten cents, but by the hour, the charge is thirty cents for one, and ten cents for each additional person.

THE CASINO.—Close by the carriage concourse, at the northern end of the mall, and east of the terrace, is a pretty stone cottage, containing an excellent restaurant.

THE RAMBLE, a rocky hill rising from the northern side of the lake, has been transformed into country freshness and beauty, by trees, of which there are; the ash, the elm, the lime, and the beech, with almost all of the coniferæ, —pines, firs, spruces, and hemlocks,—and by common wild flowers that blossom here abundantly. Wild birds build and breed freely, while swans, ducks, and cranes swim the streams of this sequestered grove, which bears within its solitudes the charms of wildness and unmolested freedom.

SCHILLER.—On a sandstone pedestal, amid

all this beauty, stands a bronze bust of the poet, a work of art modelled by C. L. Richter, and presented to the city by German residents, in 1859.

THE PARK PHAETON.—At the terrace, it will be desirable to enter one of the carriages provided by the commissioners for the purpose of conveying passengers over the entire park, for the moderate fee of twenty-five cents each. Three times during the route an opportunity will be given to stop and examine places of special interest; the Museum of Natural History, McGowan's Pass Tavern, and the Metropolitan Museum of Art. By retaining the tickets provided at starting, passengers may remain at their leisure in any of these places, as the phaetons are passing and will stop on signal.

"THE TIGRESS AND YOUNG."—At the right of the road, just west of the terrace, stands this fine group in bronze, modelled by Augustus Caine. "The Falconer," a figure of exquisite grace, executed by George Simonds, stands on a bluff at the left, near the 72d Street entrance.

THE STATUE OF DANIEL WEBSTER, by Thomas Ball, stands on a high pedestal at the junction of the west drive and the 72d Street entrance. Handsome hotels and flats line the street at the left of the park. Within the last few years, apartment houses have multiplied to such a remarkable extent, that this mode of living seems destined to become as common in New York City, as it is in Paris or Vienna.

THE AMERICAN MUSEUM OF NATURAL HISTORY, which was incorporated by the Legislature in 1869, held its first exhibition in the arsenal, when the Verreaux collection of natural history specimens, the Elliot collection of North American birds, and the entire museum of Prince Maximilian of Neuwied, were displayed.

It was not until June, 1874, that the corner-stone of the present building,—situated in Manhattan Square, between Eighth and Ninth Avenues, and 77th and 81st Streets, and connected with the park by a bridge,—was laid by General Grant. A new portion recently has been added, which is so rich in material as greatly to strengthen the effect of the architectural design,—a not very pronounced tendency to the Romanesque. These buildings form only two of many that are to be erected as the collections require them, and the liberality of the State allows.

The current expenses of this institution are paid by the city, the Board of Trustees, and private subscriptions. The Park Department, as the representative of the city and State, provides the grounds and buildings and keeps them in repair, the trustees in return furnishing the exhibits, and opening the Museum to the public, free of charge, on Wednesday, Thursday, Friday, and Saturday, of each week, from 9 A.M. until 5 P.M., and on Wednesday and Saturday evenings until ten o'clock. A bill recently passed by the Legislature, provides that the Museum be opened Sundays also.

THE HALL OF MARBLES AND ORNAMENTAL BUILDING STONES is on the first floor, the approach to which, is under the archway that divides the two flights of circular steps leading to the main entrance.

This collection, containing about fifteen hundred blocks, principally four-inch cubes, polished on the face, and variously dressed on the other sides, represents nearly every State in the Union, and includes samples of all grades of granite, limestone, marble, slate, and rocks, used for building or ornamental purposes. Foreign stones also are exhibited in this department, and it is gratifying to discover that the Idaho marble is scarcely second in quality to the best that is found in Italy; and that the State of Washington excels almost any area of similar extent in the world, in its capacity to produce the raw materials necessary to the upbuilding of improvement enterprises. This entire collection was donated by the president of the institution, Mr. Morris K. Jesup.

A LECTURE HALL, which opens from the hall of marbles, has a seating capacity of eleven hundred. During the spring and fall seasons, free public lectures are delivered two evenings in each week. A course of lectures also is given to the teachers of the city and State, and another popular course is provided for members of the institution and their friends. Public holidays also afford an opportunity for this same kind of instruction. For all of these discourses, specially prepared stereopticon plates illustrate the subjects presented.

THE JESUP COLLECTION OF WOODS.—On the same floor with the exhibit just mentioned, another hall displays over five hundred specimens of wood, arranged in botanical order, with the diameter of each tree announced by plain figures. The cuttings are transverse, oblique, and longitudinal,—one side of the specimen being polished and varnished, while the remaining portion is left in its natural state. Water-color paintings represent the foliage, flower, and fruit, of the different trees, and their native place is indicated by green spots on the map.

Among the more ordinary woods are speci-

mens of spruce, maple, ash, oak, and the red
and white cedar. The Alaskan cedar,—a wood
much sought for ship-building purposes, as it
resists the action of salt water,—also is found
in this collection, recalling to mind the country from whence it came, where a tree occasionally is hewn down which is worth as much
as two hundred acres of the government land
on which it grew. "Here are monarchs to
whom all worshipful men inevitably lift their
hats; to see one fall under the blows of steel,
or under the embrace of fire, is to experience
a pang of sorrow," said the eloquent Samuel
Wilkeson.

Two transverse sections of redwood trees,
now on their way from California, measure ten
and twenty feet in diameter, and will extend
from the floor to the ceiling, when mounted on
platforms. These will make the collection of
American woods complete. The Douglas pine,
or red fir, which attains a height of three hundred feet, is as straight as an arrow, with trunk
often nine feet in diameter. By many shipbuilders, this wood is pronounced the very best
for masts and spars, as it possesses a remarkable flexibility and tenacity of fibre.

Of the trees in California, Mr. Julius Starre
writes: "In no place is an artist or artisan
more freely rewarded than in California for-

ests. The grace of foliage and the characteristic contour of the trees glow on many a painter's canvas, but few recognize the fact that the woody fibre of the roots and trunks, when manipulated by a skilful workman, presents as charming lines and lovely colors as the most delicate flower which grows by their side."

A specimen of larch, which thrived over five centuries ago, another of hemlock, more than half as old as its predecessor, and a piece of the "Charter Oak," exhibited in a case near the door, are the greatest curiosities in this collection. An economic entomological series, illustrative of the destructive effect of insect life on vegetation, is a recent addition to this department.

THE HIGHER FORMS OF ANIMAL LIFE are represented by specimens exhibited on the second floor near the main entrance.

Here are the skeletons of Jumbo and Samson, the former the largest specimen of the African species of elephant ever seen in confinement, and the latter an importation from India. The essential external differences consist in the shape of the head and the size of the ears.

THE SEAL COLLECTION, the best in the country, is provided from the seal islands of

Alaska, the North Atlantic, and the West Indies.

THE BUFFALO CASE contains seven fine specimens surrounded by the pear cactus, the yucca, the old-man weed, and the prairie-grass.

Cats, foxes, and bears, also are in this apartment, and in the western wing are specimens of the deer, the antelope, and the camel.

Students of zoölogy find their progress greatly facilitated by the skeletons of the animals that are placed by the side of their mounted skins.

THE HALL OF BIRDS, also on the second floor, is one of the most attractive departments in the building. The collection, which is one of the finest in America, contains twelve thousand mounted specimens, besides forty thousand arranged for study.

THE COLLECTION OF MONKEYS is located on the third floor. Here will be found gorillas, baboons, and chimpanzees, arranged in cases containing fac-similes of their native haunts. The chimpanzee, "Mr. Crowley," once a prominent member of the Central Park menagerie, has a conspicuous position.

The porpoise, dolphin, whale, opossum, and kangaroo, are displayed in the wing of this floor. Also a baby hippopotamus, and a rhinoceros, that were born in the park menagerie.

THE DEPARTMENT OF FISHES AND REPTILES includes casts of American food-fishes received from the Fish Commissioner of the United States.

A COLLECTION OF BUTTERFLIES AND MOTHS is placed in the desk-cases that are ranged about the gallery of the new building. The specimens are numerous, and many of them very brilliant. Through the efforts of Mr. A. M. Palmer, who is securing subscriptions for the purpose, the Edwards entomological collection will be donated to the Museum by the citizens of New York.

The gallery of the old building is filled with American birds; among them some particularly fine groups are placed amid the trees and nests peculiar to their tribes.

THE MINERALOGICAL COLLECTION, on the fourth floor, is now one of the most valuable in the United States. It contains many fine gems, also specimens of native metallic forms, and exemplifications of the different systems of crystallization, meteorites, etc. Conspicuous in this department is the noted Tiffany collection of gems, the brilliancy and beauty of which is superior to any collection in America.

THE GEOLOGICAL COLLECTION is rich with material, principally illustrative of this country.

THE COLLECTION OF SHELLS, which is near,

is composed of a great variety of beautiful and interesting specimens, so arranged as to be studied in connection with

THE PALEONTOLOGICAL COLLECTION, containing nearly seven thousand type and figured specimens, which is the richest and most extensive assortment of American invertebrate fossils in the world.

THE DEPARTMENT OF ETHNOLOGY AND ARCHÆOLOGY.—In the upper story of the new building, a large hall contains the tools and implements of prehistoric man, as well as his articles of adornment, and of religious worship.

MODELS AND PRINTS OF THE CLIFF DWELLINGS, and old Pueblo ruins of the Verde Valley in Arizona, from which very many of these specimens were taken, form a part of this valuable collection. The States of Ohio, Arizona, and Colorado, are rich with examples of these curious structures, those of the latter State being lined with pink gypsum. It is believed that human beings will yet be found inhabiting these caverns, but as yet only skulls and other bones have been discovered. These now are exhibited with the various relics from this unknown civilization.

Antedating the cliff-dwellings, are the mounds, usually covered with a growth of trees, indicative of at least a thousand years abandonment. Many of the mound-works evidently were designed as citadels of defence, or watch-towers in war, others as places of burial for the dead, or temples of worship. As they usually resemble animals very closely in form, they are regarded as symbolizing the totems, or beasts that bore a religious significance to the tribes. Totemism appears in every land where tribes have been in existence, as, for instance, the wild ass of Issachar, the lion of Judah, etc.

One of the most remarkable of these works, the "Great Serpent" of Ohio, is situated on a hill in Adams County. The distended jaws, holding an oval one hundred and sixty feet in length, and eighty feet in width, seem to indicate that the creature is represented in the act of swallowing an egg. The mound terminates in a triple coil at the tail, the whole body extending over about seven hundred feet of ground.

The implements and ornaments found in the mounds, usually are composed of stone, and, with the exception of the flint-spears and arrowheads, are wrought with skill and care. Some of the ornaments are of copper, but always in its native state, and with the specks of silver found only in the copper of the Lake Superior region. Almost every mound contains pottery, generally coarse and crude, but sometimes graceful in form and highly ornamental. Internal commerce is indicated by masses of galena, calc-spar, quartz-crystals, mica, marine shells, and other materials brought from distant localities. There is also proof that the lead mines near Lexington, Kentucky, as well as the oil wells in Canada and Pennsylvania, were worked by the inhabitants of these queer dwelling-places. No tablets or inscriptions of any kind having been found, it is supposed that the mound-builders had no written language; and no bones have been discovered to indicate the domestication of animals.

The prehistoric remains, so abundant in Arizona, appear to be related to the civilization of Mexico, and the semi-civilized Indian tribes now found there, possibly are descendants of these ancient folk; but the mound-builders and cliff-dwellers were quite different from the nomadic Indians who occupied the country at the time of the advent of Europeans.

Among the relics contained in the Museum collection are specimens of stone, shell, pottery, pipes (that compelled the smoker to lie on his back in order to prevent the burning material from escaping), bones, materials used in the construction of the dwellings, articles of apparel, cords, weapons, and many other novel and highly instructive souvenirs of an almost mystical past.

The Library and Reading Room, now containing twenty-three thousand volumes, and with a capacity for fifty thousand more, occupies a portion of the floor just indicated. Study rooms for the use of students also are provided in this part of the building, the aim of the institution being to establish a post-graduate university of natural science, that shall be as complete in all of its appointments as any similar institution in London or Paris.

From the cariage-road, the lake, the ramble, and the belvedere,—a stone look-out tower, erected on the highest knoll in the park,—are the first objects of interest after leaving the Museum.

The Receiving-Reservoir of the Croton Water Works next comes into view, at the right of the drive. This receptacle has a capacity of one hundred million gallons. The retaining-reservoir, a little further north, holds one billion and thirty million gallons. The water supply of the city is drawn from the Croton River, a stream in Westchester County, and from a number of lakes in the vicinity of its sources.

The Equestrian Statue of General Simon Bolivar, on an elevation at the left, was a gift from the government and people of Venezuela. This work was executed by R. De la Cora.

THE DRIVE now leads through the wild beauty of woody hills and rocky slopes at the north of the park, until the second station is reached,—formerly known as Mount St. Vincent, but now called McGowan's Pass Tavern. From the porch of this attractive restaurant the eye rests, in the summer season, on brilliant flower-beds filled with the choicest plants. Far beyond are spread the waters of the East and Harlem Rivers, in which the islands, and the buildings on them, easily may be identified. A more charming spot hardly can be imagined for the nuns who, according to tradition, lived here previous to the Revolution.

CHAPTER X.

THE FIFTH AFTERNOON.

HISTORICAL SITES.—McGowan's Pass, formerly a circuitous portion of the old Boston Road, and now a park-highway in front of the tavern, was the scene of an attack by the British, at the time of the retreat of Putnam's column to Harlem Heights. A successful resistance was made by Silliman, with the aid of Alexander Hamilton, who, with his cannon, had guarded the rear of the column during the whole of its dangerous march from Bleecker Street, the British extending their lines from this point to the Hudson and East Rivers just after the American army had passed. Remains of the extensive breastworks, subsequently erected by the British, are still visible near the elevation on which the tavern stands; and at the north, on a low bluff, once called Fort Fish, an old cannon, a mortar, and a shell, are still preserved as relics of this time.

THE BLOCK HOUSE.—This fortification, to which visitors must be directed by a park-policeman, was built by the Americans, but was afterward improved and occupied by the English during Revolutionary times. Another tradition clings to the flag-staff on the summit. It is popularly called "Old Hickory," because

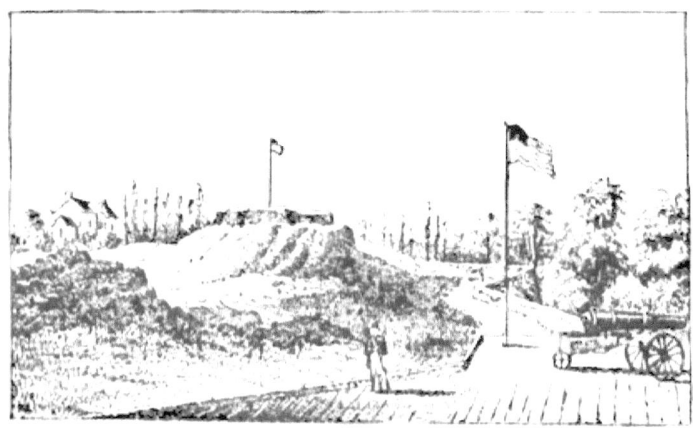

THE OLD FORT FISH AT M'GOWAN'S PASS.

General Jackson, who bore that soubriquet, is said to have once been its owner.

The vista from this point is exceptionally fine. At the north and west the Palisades, the Bloomingdale Asylum, the private mansions overlooking the Hudson, the lofty and winding elevated railroad, the ornamental stairways and battlements that constitute the first improvements of Morningside Park, Mount Morris Park, and further on Fort Washington,—the strongest breastwork thrown up by the Americans during the Revolution,— are the various objects of interest presented.

The site of the camp-fires of various regiments at different times in possession here, is a little to the left of this fort.

After leaving the tavern the phaeton passes over the east drive, which for some distance possesses no objects of special interest, except the entrance to the reservoir,—a sort of gate-house built of granite,—and

THE STATUE OF ALEXANDER HAMILTON.— This work by Charles Conradts, was presented to the city in 1880, by the son of the illustrious statesman. A monument to Hamilton once was erected in Weehawken, the place where he fought the duel with Burr; but the locality became the scene of such frequent duels, that the gentleman who raised the tribute caused it to be broken into fragments. Another fine statue of this celebrated individual was placed in the Stock Exchange in Wall Street, but the falling in of the roof, at the time of the great fire of 1835, crushed it to atoms.

THE OBELISK.—East of the drive and opposite the Metropolitan Museum of Art, stands a relic that antedates the birth of Christ by fifteen centuries. This monolith, which was gazed upon by Moses, was one of two erected for the Temple of On by Thutmes the Third, of Egypt, as a thank-offering for his victories. The hieroglyphic inscriptions mostly are commemorative of that great monarch, although the names and titles of Ramses the Second, and of Usorkon the First, also appear. The obelisk was presented to the city in 1877, by the late Khedive of Egypt, Ismail Pasha, the expense of its removal, one hundred thousand dollars, having been borne by William H. Vanderbilt. The site from which it eventually was taken was near Alexandria, it having been placed there before the Cæsarium, in the time of Augustus Cæsar. Its companion now stands in London.

THE METROPOLITAN MUSEUM OF ART.— In November 1869, at a public meeting held in the Academy of Music, a committee composed of fifty gentlemen, was formed to draft a plan of organization, for the purpose of founding an institute, the object of which should be the art culture of the people of New York City. In 1870 the Legislature granted this committee, which was then increased to over twice the original number, a charter "for the purpose of establishing a museum and library of art; of encouraging and developing the study of the fine arts; of the application of art to manufactures and to practical life; of advancing the general knowledge of kindred subjects; and to that end, of furnishing popular instruction and recreation." The Museum is controlled by a Board of Trustees, elected by the members of the corporation, who are such for life. The officers, elected annually by the corporation, are *ex-officio* members of the Board of Trustees, as are also the president of the Department of Public Parks, the comptroller of the city of New York, and the president of the National Academy of Design.

The growth of this institution has no parallel, even in countries where such effort is entirely supported by government; and, as a natural consequence, the current expenses continually increase. The trustees have spared neither their personal means, nor their time, to meet the constantly increasing demand, but it has now become so heavy that they are asking the city to assume the entire financial responsibility of the annual outlay, while they in return will open the Museum to the public, free of charge at all times, and devote their means to the enlargement and perfection of the collection.

As at the present time the Park Department furnishes accommodations for the Museum, and contributes funds for its maintainment, the trustees admit the general public on Wednesdays, Thursdays, Fridays, and Saturdays, from 10 A.M. until one half-hour before sunset; on Sundays, from 1 P.M. until the same hour, and on Tuesday and Saturday evenings, from 8 until 10 o'clock; besides this, art students and public school teachers and scholars are allowed special privileges. On the remaining days an admission fee of twenty-five cents is charged.

The technical art schools for designing, modelling, carving, free-hand and mechanical drawing, that are established in connection with the work of the Museum, add greatly to the earning capacity of this class of American laborers.

The Blodgett collection of pictures, the first acquisition of any importance, was exhibited in a rented house in Fifth Avenue, near 53d Street. After the presentation of an archæological collection, consisting of over thirty thousand objects, gathered from the Island of Cyprus by General Di Cesnola, then United States Consul, the Museum was removed to a more extensive mansion in 14th Street. The present building has been occupied since 1880, at which time it was formally opened by the President of the United States. Like the Museum of Natural History, a series of buildings is intended, two of which are completed, and a third is in process of construction. These now standing are of red brick with granite facings, but the architectural design is hard to classify, not being quite definitely the

Gothic or Renaissance that they appear to illustrate.

ANCIENT SCULPTURE.—The entrance hall is filled with casts of the greatest art productions of Greece and Rome. Here also are fragments of the bronze crabs that supported the obelisk in Alexandria. They are dated the eighteenth year of Augustus Cæsar.

THE HALL OF GLASS, LACES, ANCIENT POTTERY, AND MUSICAL INSTRUMENTS.—The large apartment at the left contains a varied assortment of rare specimens, in which the history of glass is wonderfully illustrated. Exquisite laces are displayed in swinging standards, and curious musical instruments invite the attention of those who are interested in the mechanics of sound.

THE HALL OF MODERN SCULPTURE, which is beyond the one just mentioned, contains, in a not very large assortment, the following beautiful pieces of statuary. Near the door is a life-size bronze figure of Napoleon the First, idealized by Canova's graceful touch. The majestic forms of Cleopatra, Semiramis, and Medea, by W. W. Story, are placed in line at the right of the hall, and near them are: "California" (represented as a woman of exquisite proportions), by Hiram Powers, and a beautiful group, "Latona and her Children, Apollo and Diana," by Reinhart. A cast of Antoine Louis Baryé's " Lion and Serpent," the original of which stands in the Garden of the Tuileries at Paris, is an acquisition which was presented to the United States by the French government in 1890. Thorwaldsen, Gibson, Lord Ronald Gower, and other equally noted artists, also are represented; and vases, a great variety of busts, the Poe Memorial (presented by the artists of New York), reproductions, and plaster studies, add their attractions to this part of the establishment.

THE HALL OF ARCHITECTURAL CASTS, in the interior of the building, is filled with a remarkably valuable collection, including models of ancient temples, modern cathedrals, foreign structures, and casts of every variety of detail work. A large painting by Hans Makart, called " Diana's Hunting Party," which hangs on the western wall, illustrates the high tones of the Dusseldorf School. On the eastern wall is a painting by Constant, a pupil of Cabanel's, representing " Justinian in Council."

THE OLD WESTERN GALLERIES, that are approached by a staircase leading from the Hall of Statuary, consist of two apartments in which the paintings of modern masters are displayed. These are owned by the Museum, the most noticeable treasures among them being;

"WOODLAND AND CATTLE," by Auguste Bonheur, an exquisite picture portraying a quiet phase of animal life. The sunlit landscape represents the woods of Fontainebleau.

"THUSNELDA AT THE TRIUMPHAL ENTRY OF GERMANICUS INTO ROME," by Piloty.— Although this picture is defective in its schemes of color, it is a fine piece of stage-grouping, in which barbaric figures, strange animals, trophies, and Italians, make up the glories of a Roman holiday.

BARON ALEXANDER VON HUMBOLDT.—This interesting portrait of the great *savant* at the age of eighty-nine, was painted, according to his wish, with Chimborazo for the background, by Julius Schrader.

"FRIEDLAND, 1807," by Meissonier.—The sentiment expressed in this painting is particularly fine. Napoleon at the height of his glory,—an inspiration to his soldiers, who are ready to lay down their lives at his feet,—was the intention of the artist. To quote from an eminent critic; "A painter has perhaps never represented a composition in which the leader reposes in the sympathy of his troops so like a soul in a body." The work is executed with that fidelity to detail which has seemed possible to Meissonier alone, and also with a devotion to the subject which has made of this picture the masterpiece of a great master.

"A SPANISH LADY," by Fortuny, is one of the most important specimens of the work of that artist.

"THE HORSE FAIR," by Rosa Bonheur.— This celebrated chef-d'œuvre of the distinguished artist, which represents a group of foreign draught horses in precipitate action, was presented to the museum by Cornelius Vanderbilt. It is gratifying to know that this magnificent representation of animal life is permanently placed where it may be seen by multitudes of people. Mlle. Bonheur's latest painting, "The Last of the American Indians," will be of special interest to the American public.

"THE DEFENCE OF CHAMPIGNY," by Détaille, one of the finest works the gallery contains, depicts most graphically, the harrowing scenes incident to a siege. The officer in the centre of the picture is General Faron.

MEMORIALS OF WASHINGTON, LAFAYETTE, AND FRANKLIN.—This important collection is displayed in an apartment which is situated at the head of the middle stairway, beyond the galleries just described.

THE NEW WESTERN GALLERIES that open from the room devoted to memorials, contain the paintings bequeathed to the Museum by Catharine Lorillard Wolfe.

A PORTRAIT OF MISS WOLFE, by Cabanel, attracts immediate attention by the grace of posture and air of distinguished elegance that characterized this sensitive, high-bred lady. The subtle power of the artist especially betrays itself in the modelling and posture of the hands, that express in their cultured gesture the extreme refinement manifested in our select American types.

"REPOSE IN EGYPT," by Ludwig Knaus.— This painting represents the Holy Family, visited in the night-time by a gambolling bevy of cherubs (who resemble cupids more nearly). Although Joseph appears to be in a state of religious exaltation, nothing in the picture suggests the source of his inspiration. The Virgin is a simple rustic, and the angels all possess the faces belonging to the agreeable low life that the artist usually portrays. Another specimen of Knaus in this collection is much more characteristic of that original artist.

"THE SHULAMITE WOMAN," by Cabanel, is enlivened with every device of pictorial fancy, and the theme is extremely attractive, but profound thought or spirited manipulation are wanting.

"A Religious Procession in Brittany," by Jules Breton, represents "The Grand Pardon," which is supposed by the simple-hearted Brittany peasants to occur once a year for their benefit. The composition is crowded, but the figures are skilfully generalized. "The Peasant Girl," a smaller example of Breton, is a single-figure study which is very successful.

"The Night Patrol at Smyrna," by Decamps, one of the best examples of that artist, is magnificent in its expression of light and heat, animal motion, and superb horsemanship.

"Crusaders Before Jerusalem," by Kaulbach, a repetition of a fresco in the Museum at Berlin, is an allegorical pageant, painted with great power.

"The Massacre of the Mamelukes," by Bida, "The Storm," by Cot, and "The Last Token," by Max, are noticeable features of this broadly representative collection, which is further enriched with examples of Bonheur, Bouguereau, Gérôme, Meissonier, Diaz, Munkacsy, Schreyer, Troyon, Verboeckhoven, Vibert, and many other equally noted artists.

Gallery Q, which is next to the Wolfe galleries, is filled with gems, objects wrought in gold and silver, (many of them being Egyptian, Babylonian, Assyrian, Greek or Roman), miniatures, fans of the most delicate manufacture, and exceedingly fine tapestries.

A GALLERY OF DRAWING, in which an alcove is devoted to water-color paintings, and another gallery which displays fac-similes of gold and silver plate, are at the left of Gallery Q, and lead directly to

THE NEW EASTERN GALLERY O.—This apartment contains the paintings by the old masters, that were presented to the Museum by Henry G. Marquand, the different schools being represented by the following artists:

THE DUTCH SCHOOL.—Rembrandt, the unrivalled master of chiaroscuro, whose vigor of style and truthful presentation render his works invaluable. The "Portrait of a Man with a Black Hat" is considered to be the most excellent of the four examples that the gallery contains of this artist. Teniers, the celebrated painter of interiors, Leyden, whose engravings on copper gave him rank with Dürer, and Marc Antonio, Jan Van Eyck, Franz Hals, Hoogstraaten, and Jensen, are among the other names that appear on the catalogue.

THE SPANISH SCHOOL.—Velazquez, the head of this school, of whom Ruskin has said: "Everything Velazquez does may be taken as absolutely right by the student." Among the specimens executed by this artist is one of the celebrated Don Baltasar portraits. Zurbaran, a court painter for Philip the Fourth, is the only compatriot of Velazquez here represented. Spanish art, which was an outgrowth of the Italian, achieved its greatest triumphs in the seventeenth century.

THE ITALIAN SCHOOL,—always dominantly ideal in method, and generally in subject.— Leonardo da Vinci, who in drawing from life gained a freedom unknown to other draughtsmen, and who was the first painter to recognize light and shade as equally important with the elements of color and line, Masaccio, who rendered the Brancacci Chapel famous almost beyond rivalry, and Moroni, who was second only to Titian as a portrait painter.

THE FLEMISH SCHOOL.—Peter Paul Rubens, whose brush produced more paintings than any other artist, Antony Van Dyck, a pupil of Rubens, and afterward "Painter to his Majesty," Charles the First of England. The famous portrait of the Duke of Richmond and Lenox is in this collection.

THE FRENCH SCHOOL.—In this Prud'hon, who was instructor to Empress Marie Louise, only is represented.

THE ENGLISH SCHOOL.—Turner, whose "Saltash" is here exhibited, John Constable, whose works are landscapes chiefly, Sir Joshua

Reynolds, the greatest portrait painter of England, Thomas Gainsborough, the competitor of Sir Joshua, William Hogarth, whose power to satirize found expression through grotesque forms and pictorially-displayed incidents, and Hans Holbein, the Austrian-English painter, who stands by the side of the greatest art masters of the world.

GALLERY P, which opens from the new eastern galleries, displays an assortment of American antiquities.

THE RUINS OF PAESTUM.—This remarkable mosaic, by Rinaldi, which faces the eastern middle stairway, is extremely beautiful, both in design and coloring.

"SAINT CHRISTOPHER AND THE INFANT CHRIST."—This painting faces the mosaic at a landing of the staircase. It is by Antonio Pollajuolo, and was cut from the walls of the Chapel of Michelozzi Villa in Florence.

THE OLD EASTERN GALLERIES contain pictures of the old masters, owned by the Museum, and examples of modern masters, some of which are loaned, while others are recent gifts.

"RETURN OF THE HOLY FAMILY FROM EGYPT."—This valuable picture was painted for the Church of the Jesuits at Antwerp, after the completion of the "Crucifixion," and before the "Descent from the Cross" had been executed. Grandeur of style, power of coloring, and decision, are among the expressions of praise bestowed upon it by the catalogues.

PORTRAITS OF THE HONORABLE HENRY FANE AND HIS GUARDIANS, INIGO JONES AND CHARLES BLAIR, by Sir Joshua Reynolds.— This picture is one of the best examples of the famous painter, and one of the most valuable acquisitions to a collection which includes specimens from Correggio, the school of Fra Bartholommeo, Dürer, Del Sarto, Velazquez, Van Dyck, Teniers, Maas, Lely, Jordaens, Greuze, and many others.

"COLUMBUS BEFORE FERDINAND AND ISABELLA," by Brozick, "Reading Homer," by Alma Tadema,—that careful painter who has attained such perfection in the historical details of dress and architecture,—"Wallenstein's Lager," by Messerschmitt, which was awarded the highest prize at the Royal Academy in Munich in 1887, "Joan of Arc," by Bastien LePage, a pupil of Cabanel's, portraits of Washington and John Jay, by Stuart, Alexander Hamilton, by Trumbull, Bayard Taylor, by Eastman Johnson, and Walt Whitman, by Alexander, constitute the most important paintings in the second department.

Two balconies that connect the eastern with

the western galleries exhibit specimens of Oriental porcelain and Japanese art.

"LIONS CHASING DEER," by Rubens, "Alexander and Diogenes," by Gaspard de Crayer, "Returning from the Hunt," by Josef Horemans, are three of the paintings that occupy the hallway which leads from the old eastern galleries to the floor below.

The success of the Museum, and the superior quality of paintings which it exhibits, demonstrates the remarkable progress that our country has made in its patronage and appreciation of art during the past quarter of a century. This institution, and the private galleries from which paintings constantly are being loaned by their generous owners, possess examples of the greatest artists of ancient and modern times, and these are, many of them, the very best examples. As the general public is permitted frequent access to these potent agents of civilization, the stimulus necessarily must permanently increase, and it is to be hoped that the day is not far distant when our importation of this class of foreign work may not be impeded by a tariff.

The corridors at the eastern side of the lower floor are filled with a great variety of relics from Assyria, Babylon, Egypt, and other foreign countries. Many of these are mortuary, and include mummies and mummy-cases, sarcophagi, etc. A part of the Cesnola collection is placed with these curiosities, the remaining portion being divided and scattered about the building.

THE PHAETON TO FIFTH AVENUE ENTRANCE.—The first object to attract attention after leaving the Museum will be the new Jewish syngaogue in Fifth Avenue, at 76th Street. The beauty of this edifice, which is classical Renaissance in its design, is much impaired by the gilded frame and black panels of its dome.

"THE PILGRIM," by J. Q. A. Ward, is a bronze statue, well placed on a rise of ground at the left of the drive, but not seen to advantage, because the phaeton turns to the right just before it is reached. This attractive representation of our forefathers was a gift from the New England Society.

A STATUE OF S. B. MORSE, by Byron Picket, stands east of the 72d Street entrance. It was erected by telegraphers, in 1871.

The other statues in the park, not seen from the phaeton are; "Commerce" by Guion, Mazzini, the Italian agitator, by Turini, and the Seventh Regiment Monument, by Ward. The latter is a bronze figure of a private soldier in the Seventh Regiment, erected in commemoration of the comrades who fell during the Civil War. A statue of Columbus, presented by Italian residents, is to be placed on the plaza, at 110th Street and Fifth Avenue, and a statue of Thorwaldsen is another addition which is proposed as a present from Danish residents.

CHAPTER XI.

THE SIXTH MORNING.—THE ISLANDS.

LIBERTY, OR BEDLOE'S ISLAND, on which stands Bartholdi's great statue, "Liberty Enlightening the World," is situated in New York Bay, about two miles southwest of the Battery. From 8 A.M. until 4 P.M. boats leave hourly for this destination from the Barge Office pier.

During the later days of the colonial epoch these thirteen acres of island property belonged to Captain Archibald Kennedy, then Collector of the Port, whose summer residence was situated in this delightful spot; but after the Revolution a series of transformations took place, the State first utilizing it as a quarantine station, and Government afterward converting it into a military fortification, which in turn yielded its possession to the imperial goddess who keeps watch over our destinies at the present time. The star-shaped, granite walls of Fort Wood still remain, forming a rather ornamental inclosure for the pedestal. As a military post this island only has been put to practical service, when, during the Rebellion, a number of buildings were erected and used as hospitals.

When, many years ago, Bartholdi, the

THE BARTHOLDI STATUE OF LIBERTY.

French sculptor, entered the port of New York, he was so greatly impressed with the eagerness of the emigrants, who crowded on deck to obtain a first glimpse of the land of freedom and opportunity, that he conceived the idea of symbolizing by a statue of Liberty, the welcome that foreigners received.

It was not until after the close of the Civil War, at a social meeting of prominent Frenchmen in Paris,—on which occasion Bartholdi was present,—that the idea of presenting the statue to America was first advanced, and received with an amount of enthusiasm which insured the completion of the project. Subscriptions subsequently were received to the extent of over a million of francs, and the work was finished and conveyed to our shores in the month of June, 1885. As the sympathy of France for this country demonstrated itself by the assistance of a valiant contingent, in our time of great struggle for independence, so that bond of interest again found expression by a gift commemorative of our success, and suggestive of the possibilities of our future. Two hundred and fifty thousand dollars having been obtained for a pedestal (through the efforts of the New York *World*) the statue was unveiled on the 28th of October 1886, in the presence of the President and many distinguished guests, with imposing ceremonies, elaborate decorations, and the booming of cannon.

This largest statue of modern times is one hundred and fifty-one feet in height. In one hand the figure holds a tablet, while with the other she uplifts a torch. The body is gracefully draped, and the head is surmounted by a diadem. The material is hammered copper. A spiral stairway within the statue, leads to the head, where forty persons can stand together without material inconvenience. Another stairway in the arm leads to the torch-chamber. No elevators are provided, and the climb is very trying, but the view afforded from the top is magnificent. At night the torch is lighted by electricity, and the base and pedestal also are illuminated. The forefinger of the right hand of the goddess is seven feet in length, and at the second joint, four feet in circumference. The nose is over three feet long, and the statue weighs over twenty-five tons. The extreme height above low-water mark is nearly three hundred and six feet. The pedestal, constructed of granite and concrete, is one hundred and fifty-five feet in height. This colossus can be seen from a distance of many miles.

ELLIS ISLAND, once known as Bucking Island, contained, until 1827, a small circular fort, called Fort Gibson. The five acres that constitute this plot of ground belong to the

United States, and have been used as a place of storage for explosives. At the present time government officials here receive immigrants in the landing depot, which was formally opened on New Year's Day, 1892. The wooden structure erected for this purpose, nearly covers the island, is three stories in height, and has a tower at each corner. The cost of construction was almost half a million dollars. The first floor is devoted to baggage-transfer and local express offices, as well as to the private offices of the government express. At the landing of a ship the newcomers are received on the second floor, the crowd pouring over the gang-plank in a compact mass, pushing, jabbering, gesticulating. Officers calmly direct the bewildered strangers to desks, where name, place of birth, age, occupation, and destination, are registered. Everything here is so perfectly systematized that from twelve to fifteen thousand immigrants easily can be handled at one time, twelve lines being formed, with a registry clerk in attendance at each line. From a gallery in this room the public may view the motley procession. On this floor there are also rooms for the detention of paupers, lunatics, criminals, and persons suspected of being contract laborers. Women and children are provided with separate apartments, and a telegraph station, money exchange, postal station, information bureau, and railroad and steamship office are in convenient arrangement. The third floor contains sleeping rooms for the accommodation of immigrants who are detained over night. None of the officials reside on the island except the surgeon.

A ferryboat continually plies between Ellis Island and the Barge Office, and visitors are permitted at any time.

The greatest number of immigrants landed in New York in one year, was four hundred and fifty-five thousand, four hundred and fifty. This was in 1883. The greatest number landed in one day was on May 11th, 1887, when nearly sixteen thousand were registered. Of late years the immigration from Italy has far exceeded that of any other country.

GOVERNOR'S ISLAND.—This egg-shaped plot of ground, containing nearly sixty-five acres, is situated about one thousand yards south of the Battery. It was first purchased from the Indians by Wouter Van Twiller, the second Dutch governor of New York, and that worthy personage whom Irving describes as having weighed the books of disputing merchants to discover if their accounts would not balance. The Indian name of the island was "Pagganek," or Nut Island, for some time called Nutten Island, but after it became the Van Twiller residence it was known as Governor's Island, and has retained that appellative.

Since the War of 1812, at which time the batteries now found on it were erected, this property has been exclusively under the control of the United States War Department. It is now headquarters for the Military Department of the Atlantic, and the Major-General and his staff are residents. The northern portion of the island is occupied by the Ordnance Department as the New York Arsenal. Cannon balls are ranged about it in pyramids, and on the little wharf is one of the largest guns owned by the Government. The parade-ground is adorned with fine old shade-trees, and the residences of officers. A chapel erected by the widow of General Hancock, the library and picture gallery of the Military Service Institution, and the Military Museum, which contains battle-flags and other war relics, are interesting social features of the present occupation. A footpath leads to Fort Columbus, the stone fortification in the centre of the island, now utilized as quarters for the soldiers. Castle William, an old-fashioned stone work, with three tiers of casemates, is located on the northwestern shore. In the haste incident to the War of 1812, even the professors and students from college and school were called upon to assist in the completion of this prominent fortress. A small triangular battery and two magazines are situated on the southern point of the island, and everything is in preparation for the rapid throwing up of earthworks and the mounting of heavy guns, Castle William being considered entirely too old-fashioned to withstand the fire from modern ships-of-war.

CHAPTER XII.

THE SIXTH AFTERNOON.—A SAIL ON THE EAST RIVER.

The Jersey City Ferry at the foot of Cortlandt Street, where also is the dock for the Glen Island boat, was the one for which Robert Fulton built the two boats, the "York" and the "Jersey," in 1812.

After leaving its pier the steamer must first round the Battery, the southern terminus of Manhattan Island. At the west and south lie the Ellis and Bedloe Islands, and the shores of New Jersey, whereon the Jersey City docks are more conspicuous than pleasing. Robin's Reef Lighthouse is below these, on a reef of rocks that once was a resort for seals.

STATEN ISLAND, at the south, is a richly wooded and hilly tract of country, containing about sixty square miles of land that are occupied chiefly by the villas of New York business men. A point of the eastern shore forms, with the western coast of Long Island, the Narrows, or entrance to New York Harbor,—a passage protected by Fort Wadsworth and a line of water batteries on the Staten Island side, and by the two forts, Hamilton and Lafayette, on the opposite shore.

Staten Island was purchased from the Indians in 1657, for ten shirts, thirty pairs of stockings, ten guns, thirty bars of lead, thirty pounds of powder, twelve coats, twelve pieces of duffel, thirty hatchets, twenty hoes, and a case of knives.

New York Harbor is a body of water about nine miles in length and three miles in width. From the ocean at Sandy Hook to the metropolis at the head of the bay it is about twenty-eight miles. No city in the world has a more majestic approach or a more agreeable situation. The waters of its harbor are deep enough to float the largest vessels, and from their contiguity to the ocean, are never frozen in the winter. The wide expanse of the lower and upper bays, the wooded slopes that form at once a shelter and a picture of rare beauty, the islands, and the rivers that, like encircling arms, hold in their caress the fairest city of the freest country on the earth, and the proud city itself,—uplifting spires and domes on stately buildings that tell of prosperous times and unexampled greatness of achievement,—enthuse and melt the heart of the returning patriot, or inspire with new sense of possibility the mind of the foreigner who watches from the deck of an incoming steamer this panorama of nature and display of human progress.

Quarantine Station is on the eastern coast of Staten Island. Governor's Island, which will be remembered, is separated from Long Island by Buttermilk Channel, east of which are located the docks and piers of South Brooklyn. The New York shore, for a considerable distance along the East River, is crowded with merchant ships from every country, river and sound steamers, and ferryboats loaded with passengers, plying between two of the busiest of cities.

THE WHARFAGE FACILITIES OF NEW YORK excel those of any city in the world, and the cost of handling the cargoes is much less than in Liverpool or London. Over one hundred steamers, belonging to the trans-Atlantic fleet, ply between New York and European ports. Twenty distinct lines, exclusive of the local, are in operation between this and the coast and Gulf ports. The yearly average of foreign vessels entered during the last five years is eight thousand. The number of vessels received and despatched annually aggregates about thirty-four thousand. The imports of merchandise in 1631 amounted to about twenty-three thousand dollars; the exports in the same year, twenty-seven thousand dollars. In the year 1891 nearly six million dollars' worth of merchandise was received, and nearly four million dollars' worth of material was exported. The first wharf was constructed in 1648, when the population of New York numbered less than one thousand. In 1687 the total shipping amounted to but three ships and fifteen sloops and barks. In 1807 Fulton's steamboat, the "Clermont," made its first trip to Albany, in thirty-two hours. The first steamship, the "Savannah," crossed the Atlantic in 1819, taking twenty-five days, the usual time for fast clipper-ships having been from sixteen to twenty-one days.

JEANNETTE PARK is a small space between Pearl Street and the river, above Broad Street, —formerly designated "Coenties Slip," in honor of an influential Dutch shoemaker whose shop once occupied a corner in this locality. Here stood the clumsy stone tavern, or city hall, of the Dutch administration. A corporation pier, erected at this point in 1751, was the first public improvement for which money was borrowed, the bond given having borne an interest of six per cent.

The water front, from the Battery to Fulton Street, is artificially-made ground, the natural riverside having been at Pearl Street, along which the little village of New Amsterdam first extended itself. This was a favorite locality for markets, the old "Fly Market" having

THE OLD STADTHUYS.

been the most celebrated. The Dutch word *vly*, meaning valley, was the original appellation. Near Fulton Street the first ferry to Long Island was established in 1638, a small skiff having been used to convey the passengers, who sometimes had to wait an entire day before crossing.

BROOKLYN BRIDGE, the history and proportions of which already have been described, spans the East River as it bends eastward, and is seen to great advantage from the boat.

A little distance beyond, at the Brooklyn side, the steamer passes the United States Navy Yard, situated in Wallabout Bay, the name of which is a corruption of "Waale

Boght." The United States Naval Lyceum and the United States Marine Hospital are located at this point. Preparations for ship-building are conducted within the enormous sheds near the river; the cob-dock occupies the bay.

CORLEAR'S HOOK.—This point of land, below Grand Street and opposite the Navy Yard, has been called Corlear's Hook since Stuyvesant granted the property to one sturdy Van Corlear, for faithful services rendered. In 1643 a number of Indians having encamped at this place, awakened the fear of the white settlers, who surprised the red men at mid-

THE FIRST FERRY FROM NEW YORK TO LONG ISLAND.

night, killing over thirty and inflicting atrocious barbarities. This action was the direct cause of the revolt of eleven tribes of previously peaceful Indians. The locality now is headquarters for the most daring river thieves.

BELLEVUE HOSPITAL, at 26th Street, is easily discerned from the river. The Morgue, where dead bodies are left for identification, is near the water's edge.

KIP'S BAY.—According to Washington Irving, this indentation at the foot of 36th Street received its name from the following adventure: " . . . At the bow of the commodore's boat was stationed a very valiant man named Hendrick Kip. . . . No sooner did he behold these varlet heathens" (Indians) "then he trembled with excessive valor, and although a good half mile distant, he seized a musketoon that lay at hand and, turning away his head, fired it most intrepidly in the face of the blessed sun. The blundering weapon recoiled and gave the valiant Kip an ignominious kick, which laid him prostrate with uplifted heels in the bottom of the boat. But such was the effect of this tremendous fire that the wild men of the woods, struck with consternation, seized hastily upon their paddles and shot away into one of the deep inlets of the Long Island shore.

"This signal victory gave new spirits to the voyagers; and in honor of the achievement they gave the name of the valiant Kip to the surrounding bay."

It was here that the British landed when, in September 1776, they made their first attack on Washington's army, and caused the precipitate retreat of American soldiers stationed at this point.

LONG ISLAND CITY, which begins directly opposite Kip's Bay, and extends northward for a considerable distance, comprises the formerly separated districts of Ravenswood, Astoria, and Hunter's Point,—a locality occupied by oil-refineries and factories. The former sections, however, contain country villas and handsome residences, and do not in reality fuse with their hardworking sister.

BLACKWELL'S ISLAND.—This long and narrow strip of land, the next point of interest on the route, was once the country seat of John Manning, the captain in charge of the fort at the time of its capture by the Dutch in 1673. A more delightful place of residence scarcely can be imagined. Graceful in form, with moss-covered rocks, swaying trees, flowers, and abundance of greensward, this charming island was a home of which its owner might well be proud. It was not until 1828 that the city purchased the property for its charitable and correctional institutions.

These now include the charity hospital, penitentiary, almshouse, hospital for incurables, female lunatic asylum, convalescent hospital, workhouse, and blind asylum. The buildings all have been constructed of stone quarried from the island by convict labor; the general style of architecture is somewhat feudal in its character. Residences occupied by the officials in charge are surrounded with lawns and gardens, that are kept in perfect order by the inmates of the prison, almshouse, etc. These individuals also farm certain portions of this fertile land, row the officials and their families to and from the city, and have built and kept in repair the heavy granite sea-wall that protects the shores of the entire one hundred and twenty acres of land.

HELL GATE.—This celebrated strait is entered shortly after leaving Blackwell's Island. By reason of numerous rocks, shelves, and whirlpools,—known under the various appellations of "Flood Rock," "Negrohead," "Gridiron," "Hogsback" (on which his satanic majesty often was seen astride), "Fryingpan," (in which the same well-known individual always cooked his fish before a storm), "Pot Rock," etc.,—this narrow passage was very dangerous to shipping, and only could be entered with skilful pilots. Since 1876, however, the channel has been opened, the United States Government having expended nearly two millions of dollars to render it safe. The final explosion of this great work occurred at Flood Rock in 1885, at which time over fifty-two thousand pounds of dynamite were used.

WARD'S ISLAND, at the left of Hell Gate, contains about two hundred acres of ground owned by the city, the Commissioners of Emigration, and private individuals. Under the care of the city are the insane asylums for males, and the homœopathic hospital here located. A lunatic asylum, houses of refuge, and a hospital and nursery for children, constitute the buildings in which sick and destitute aliens are cared for. There is also a home for invalid soldiers who served in the regiments raised by the city during the late war. These buildings are all substantial, and some of them are highly ornamental. Groves of fine old shade trees cover portions of these structures, adding greatly to the appearance of the island. A sea-wall, which was constructed by convicts from Blackwell's Island, also girts this property. The grading and general improvements have been done by this same class of labor.

RANDALL'S ISLAND, which lies between Ward's Island and the mainland, consists of one hundred acres of city property, handsomely laid out and ornamented with shade trees. An idiot asylum, nursery, hospital, and schools, are placed here by the city, in order to provide for the wants of its destitute children. A house of refuge, under the charge of the Society for the Reformation of Juvenile Delinquents, is at the southern end of the island. In this institution children who have been

RANDALL'S ISLAND.

sentenced by the city magistrates are taught to work, as well as instructed in all the common-school branches. Passes must be obtained from the Commissioners of Public Charities and Correction, in their building at the corner of Third Avenue and 11th Street, in order to visit any of the institutions on these last-mentioned islands. A special permit is required for the lunatic asylum on Ward's Island. A ferry conveys passengers to these localities from the foot of East 26th Street.

THE CHANNEL at the south of Randall's Island, is called Little Hell Gate, the one at the north is the Bronx Kills. Several islands lie clustered within the embrace of the Westchester and Long Island shores, where the waters of the Sound begin. A fort at Throgg's Neck, and another one at Willet's Point, command this entrance to New York. Along the northern shore is Pelham Bay Park, a tract of land containing seventeen hundred acres of beautifully wooded territory, recently purchased by the city.

CITY ISLAND is noted as the place where American oyster culture first began. Hart's Island belongs to New York City, and is occupied by the Potter's Field, a branch workhouse, and a lunatic asylum. David's Island was purchased by the Government in 1869, but was used as a hospital-station during the War of the Rebellion. It is now a receiving-station for recruits.

GLEN ISLAND.—At this picturesque resort it will be fitting to terminate the labors and pleasures of the week. Rest and refreshment will be found in cool groves filled with choice varieties of rare exotics; and the return to

busier haunts will be at the close of the day,
when the weary traveller, having learned the
history of its events and the institutions of its
present time, can be content to view in the
half-light, the city which promises such stores
of wealth for the sightseer of the future.

Fold-out Place

This fold-out is being digitized, and at a future date.

old-out Placeholder

fold-out is being digitized, and will be inserted at a future date.

CHRONOLOGICAL SKETCHES OF THE CITY OF NEW YORK.

1524.—The Island of Manhattan was discovered by John De Verrazzani, a Florentine.

1609.—Hendrik (or Henry) Hudson, a navigator in the service of the States General of Holland, and the second discoverer of Manhattan Island, sailed up the Hudson River to a point a little below Albany.

1611.—The first ships that carried merchandise from the North River, the "Little Fox," and the "Little Crane," were sent from Holland on a voyage of speculation.

Three more vessels were at this time fitted out for the purpose of establishing trading posts on the Hudson River, where furs might be collected, thus saving time for the ships that crossed the ocean. One of these was called "The Tiger," the other two bore the name of "The Fortune."

The first vessel built on the shores of New York Harbor, and the first to pass through Hell-Gate, was called the "Restless," and may be considered as peculiarly entitled to honorable mention, because it was the means of filling many important blanks in the geography of the world.

1613.—Captain Adrien built four small houses and established a fur agency at what is now No. 41 Broadway.

1614.—An expedition from South Virginia, dispatched by Sir Thomas Dale, took possession of the infant colony.

Later in the year, Holland, having regained possession of the Island, sent an expedition of five vessels, that explored the whole length of Long Island, passed up the Hudson and Delaware Rivers, and were given the exclusive right to trade between the Delaware and Connecticut Rivers for three years.

1623.—A charter, under the title of the West India Company, went into operation.

This is considered to have been the era of the permanent settlement of New Netherlands.

1624.—Peter Minuit arrived at Manhattan, in the capacity of Director-General of New Netherlands, and organized a provisional government.

1625.—Three ships and a yacht from Holland, brought a number of settlers and one hundred head of cattle.

1626.—Manhattan Island was purchased from the Indians, for trinkets worth twenty-four dollars.

1633.—The first schoolmaster arrived from Holland.

The first ship-of-war, " De Soutberg" (the Salt Mountain), brought a company of soldiers to garrison the stronghold that had just been completed on the southern point of the Island.

1638.—The first ferry crossed the East River to Long Island.

1642.—A church, built of rock stone, which cost about one thousand dollars, was erected within the walls of the fort.

The first tavern, "Staadt Herberg," was built by the Dutch West India Company at Coenties Slip.

1643.—The first deed recorded was for a lot thirty by one hundred feet, that was sold for nine dollars and fifty cents.

The wreck of the ship "Princess" occurred in Bristol Channel. This was one of the most notable maritime events in connection with the early history of the city, eighty passengers, including the Director-General Kieft, and Dominie Bogardus, the first clergyman established in this city, having been drowned.

Lots were freely given to whoever would build in the town.

1648.—The first wharf was constructed.

The first ordinance for the prevention of fire was passed, after which four fire-wardens, or chimney-inspectors, were appointed.

The settlement contained twelve retail dealers.

1650.—The first lawyer, Dick Van Schelluyne, commenced practice.

1651.—All persons who were absent from the city four months lost their burgher rights.

1652.—The city of New Amsterdam was incorporated.

The first public school was established in the "Stadthuys."

1654.—Burgomasters received one hundred and forty dollars, and the Schepens one hundred dollars per annum, for their services.

1655.—Negroes were purchased from slave-ships and taken to Virginia.

1656.—New Amsterdam contained one thousand inhabitants, one hundred and twenty houses, and seventeen streets.

The first survey of the city was confirmed by law,

1657.—The English language was first recognized in New Amsterdam.

1658.—Stone pavements were laid. The street first paved still retains its former name of Stone Street.

The first fire-company, which consisted of eight men, was organized.

Whipping with a rod, and banishment from the city, was at this time the punishment for theft.

Hogs running at large, were required to have rings in their noses.

1659.—The first shipwreck on this coast, of which there is any account, occurred near Fire Island. The name of the ship was "Prince Maurice."

Poor-boxes were customarily introduced at weddings.

Houses were rented for twenty-seven dollars per annum.

The first public auctioneer was appointed. One dollar and ten cents was the fee paid for the disposal of a lot.

1660.—The establishment of a brick-yard was a notable event in connection with the architectural progress of the city. Before this time bricks had been imported from Holland, and were considered too expensive to be used, except in the construction of chimneys and ovens.

A man living near the Bowery, offered to give away his property, for the reason that he disliked to ride through two miles of dense forest to reach his work.

It was punishable to call magistrates blockheads, on account of an adverse decision.

1663.—The first suicide recorded in the town was that of a blacksmith, who hung himself from a tree near Collect Pond.

1664.—New Amsterdam was captured by the English, and its name was changed to New York.

Notice was given of a re-organization of the municipal government under the direction of Mayor, Aldermen, and Sheriff.

1665.—The first Court of Admiralty, organized by Governor Nichols, was convened and held in the Stadthuys.

1670.—A seal of the city was presented by the Duke of York.

Staten Island was purchased for a few trinkets.

The first New York Exchange was established, the members arranging to meet every Friday morning, between eleven and twelve o'clock, at the bridge which crossed the ditch at Broad Street, a locality now known as Exchange Place.

1673.—A Dutch fleet recaptured the city, in the name of the States General of Holland, and changed its name to New Orange.

The first mail between Boston and New York was established, "for a more speedy intelligence and despatch of affairs." The letters were carried by a messenger who made the round trip once a month.

At this time the main portion of the town extended from the high ridge of ground at Broadway, to the East River, then called Salt River. A great dock for vessels, and three crescent-shaped forts, were placed along the shore. Almost all of the houses presented gable ends to the street.

1674.—A treaty of peace having been signed by England and Holland, New York was again restored to the English.

Only one Jew and one Spaniard held property in the city at this period.

1677.—New York contained three hundred and forty-three houses.

1679.—A bear was killed in an orchard near Maiden Lane.

The first classis was formed, at the suggestion of the governor, for the purpose of examining and ordaining a young Bachelor in Divinity, who had been called to the church at Newcastle.

1683.—The city was divided into six wards.

The "Court of General Sessions of the Peace of the city of New York," first called the "Court of General Quarter Sessions," was instituted under royal government.

1686.—The "Dongan Charter," the basis of all later charters obtained for this city, was granted by James the Second. This declared that New York City thenceforth should comprise the entire Island of Manhattan.

The best house in the city was sold for three thousand and five hundred dollars.

1689.—Information of the accession of William and Mary, to the throne was received in New York with great satisfaction. The garrison was seized by about fifty inhabitants, who formed themselves into a committee of safety to hold the province in rule until a government could be established by the new sovereigns. This movement inaugurated a bitter strife between factions of the citizens, who contended for the temporary control, and resulted in the ascendency of Leisler.

1691.—The first Assembly met April 9th.
Leisler was tried and executed.
1692.—The first Post Office was established.
A whipping-post, pillory, and ducking-stool, were placed near the City Hall.
1693.—The first printing press was put in operation.
1696.—Trinity Church Corporation erected its first edifice.
The city contained five hundred and ninety-four houses and six thousand inhabitants.
The Reformed Protestant Dutch Church received a charter of incorporation.
1697.—The first almanac was published.
1700.—The second City Hall was erected at the corner of Nassau and Wall Streets.
1703.—The "King's Farm," a region of country extending northward from Cortlandt Street, was granted to Trinity Church Corporation by Queen Anne. This gift laid the foundation for the revenues of that society.
1709.—A slave market was established at the foot of Wall Street.
1710.—The total annual income of the city was two hundred and ninety-four pounds sterling. The total expenses were two hundred and seventy-four pounds.
A post-office establishment for the colonies in America was created by an Act of Parliament, the chief office of which was in New York.
1712.—The negro inhabitants formed a plot to set fire to the city, and in its execution killed several white persons. Nineteen of the incendiaries were convicted and executed.
1719.—The first Presbyterian Church was erected in Wall Street.

1720.—Clocks were first introduced, time having previously been recorded by hour-glasses.
1725.—The first newspaper, called the *New York Gazette*, was published.
1729—A City Library was founded.
1730.—The charter upon which the city's present system of government is based, was granted by Governor Montgomery.

A line of stages, that made bi-monthly trips, was established between New York and Philadelphia.

The first fire-engines used in the city arrived from London. A fire-department was at once organized.

1732.—The first stage from New York to Boston made the round trip once a month.
1734.—A Poor-House, and a Calaboose for unruly slaves, were erected on the Commons, now City-Hall Park.
1740.—The New York Society-Library was organized.
1741.—The famous delusion, known as the "Negro Plot," in which a large number of negroes, and a Catholic priest, were executed without cause, occasioned much excitement.
1750.—The first theatre was opened in Nassau Street.
1754.—King's College obtained a charter of incorporation.
1756.—The first ferry plied between New York and Staten Island.
1757.—The city contained about twelve thousand inhabitants.
1761.—A second theatre was opened in Beekman Street.
1763.—Light first gleamed from the Sandy Hook lighthouse.

A ferry was established between New York and Paulus Hook,—now Jersey City.

1765.—The famous Stamp-Act Congress convened in this city. Delegates were present from all the colonies, and a bold declaration of rights and grievances was adopted. An agreement not to import goods from Great Britain, until the Stamp Act was repealed, was signed by a large concourse of merchants, and a society of individuals, who called themselves the "Sons of Liberty," was organized, with affiliations throughout the country. Great excitement prevailed, and a riot occurred, in which the governor was burned in effigy, and the citizens threatened to storm the fort.

1766.—News of the repeal of the Stamp Act reached the city May 20th.

The Methodist Episcopal Society of the United States was founded by Philip Embury, in his own house in this city.

1768.—A Chamber of Commerce was organized at Queen's Head Tavern, the building afterward known as "Fraunce's Tavern."

1770.—The New York Chamber of Commerce was incorporated by the Legislature.

A statue of William Pitt was erected in William Street.

1772.—Umbrellas were imported from India. They were at first scouted as an effeminacy.

1774.—A vessel called the "Nancy" was not permitted to land her cargo of tea, nor to make entry at the Custom-House.

A Committee of Correspondence was organized, and a "Congress of Colonies" was insisted upon by the merchants.

Resolutions of resistance were adopted by

a great meeting on the Commons, now City-Hall Park.

1775.—The Colonial Assembly adjourned.

Delegates were elected to the Continental Congress.

The first New York water-works were established.

1776.—The militia was called into service in January. In the spring following, the city was in the possession of the American Army.

The leaden statue of George the Third was pulled down July 9th.

The Declaration of Independence was read from the balcony of the old City Hall, July 18th.

The king's coat-of-arms was taken from the court-room and burned on the same day.

The city was captured by the British, August 26th, after the battle of Long Island.

A great fire destroyed Trinity Church and nearly five hundred houses, September 21st.

Nathan Hale was executed as a spy, by command of General Howe.

1777.—Congress directed the Board of War to write to the government of New York, urging that the lead mines in that State be worked, and promising to supply prisoners of war for the purpose; the scarcity of lead making it necessary to use gutters and roofs, and the leaden statue of King George the Third, for bullets.

1778.—The British evacuated Philadelphia, and an army of twelve thousand men marched from that city to New York. The baggage and stores, with some three thousand non-combatants who held to their British allegiance, were sent to New York by water.

1779.—While the city was in the possession of the British, counterfeiting Continental bills was a regular business; flags of truce were made use of to put it in circulation, and the newspapers openly advertised it.

On the 19th of May, at eleven in the morning, a darkness, which continued for several hours, necessitating candles at noon-day, fell over the city. The cause of this remarkable phenomenon has been assigned to prodigious fires, that had been raging in the States of Massachusetts, Vermont, and New Hampshire.

1780.—A great scarcity of fuel and fresh provisions caused general consternation. Fruit trees were cut down, wood was twenty dollars a cord, corn was four dollars, and potatoes were two dollars a bushel. As the ice in the Hudson River offered an opportunity for the Americans to cross it, an attack upon the city was feared, and all the inhabitants were put under arms.

Four newspapers were published during the time of the British occupation, the proprietors arranging their issues so that one paper was provided for each day.

1783.—The British evacuated the city November 25th, and General Washington entered at the head of the American Army.

1785.—Congress moved from Philadelphia to New York, and convened in the City Hall, which then stood at the corner of Wall and Nassau Streets, now occupied by the United States Sub-Treasury Building.

The Bank of New York and a manumission society were established.

The first daily paper was published under the name of the *New York Daily Advertiser*.

1786.—The first city directory was issued. It contained eight hundred and forty-six names.
1787.—King's College was re-incorporated as Columbia College.
1788.—The Constitution of the United States was adopted by New York State. A great parade celebrated that event in this city
1789.—The first Congress under the Constitution of the United States, assembled in Federal Hall on the 4th of March, at which time George Washington was unanimously elected President.

The inauguration of Washington, as President of the United States, took place April 30th, on the gallery of the old City Hall.

Martha Washington held her first reception May 29th.

Tammany Society, or the Columbian Order, was founded.
1790.—The first sidewalks were laid.
1795.—Park Theatre was erected.
1797.—The "Medical Repository," the first scientific periodical printed in this country, was published.
1799.—The Manhattan Company, organized for the purpose of supplying the city with water, obtained its charter. The Bronx River, proposed as the source of supply, was surveyed.

The second bank, the Manhattan Company, was established at No. 23 Wall Street.
1800.—Collect Pond was filled in. This body of fresh water, situated on the present site of the Tombs, was of such great depth that several contractors, who engaged to fill it, were said to have become bankrupt in their efforts to do so. Many times earth rose above its level in the evening, but the next morning's

sun shone again on sparkling waters, the debris having disappeared beneath its surface.

On its western borders, surrounded by groves of trees and blackberry wilds, once was situated an Indian village, no doubt the home of the Manhattans. Fish were abundant in the pond for more than one hundred years after the Christian settlement of the Island, and one of its promontories was so abundantly strewn with a deposit of shells that the Dutch named it "Kalchook," or "Lime Shell Point." The water was of unusual purity, the celebrated Tea-water Spring having been one of its many fountains, and a number of brooks that flowed to both rivers, formed picturesque outlets for its seemingly inexhaustible supply. Doubtless the stoppage of these springs had much to do with the subsequent epidemics of yellow fever that occasioned so much mourning throughout the city.

1801.—The real and personal property of the city and county was valued at $21,964,037, and a tax was laid of one mill on the dollar.

The *Evening Post* issued its first number.

1804.—Alexander Hamilton was killed in a duel with Aaron Burr.

Sunday-schools were established.

Hackney coaches were licensed.

The first recorder of New York City was appointed.

Some alterations in the franchise having opened elections to the participation of a large number, whom property restrictions had previously prevented from having a voice in the choice of the city magistrates, this year, for the first time, witnessed a Republican majority in the Board.

1805.—Fort Clinton was erected.

The New York Free School was incorporated.

1806.—Steam navigation was successfully demonstrated by Robert Fulton.

The New York Orphan Asylum Society was founded. Mrs. Sarah Hoffman and Mrs. Alexander Hamilton were the first and second directresses.

1807.—The city was surveyed and laid out, by a commission appointed by the Legislature, in which Gouverneur Morris, DeWitt Clinton, and other prominent persons were active members.

The city contained thirty-one benevolent institutions.

A College of Physicians and Surgeons was chartered.

Washington Irving, distinguished as a heedless law-student, was admitted to the bar.

1808.—The American Academy of Fine Arts was incorporated.

1811.—The first ferry carried passengers to Hoboken.

1812.—War was declared against Great Britain.

Steam was utilized on the Jersey City ferryboats.

The manufacture of pins was inaugurated in the city by English workmen, who procured one dollar a paper for their product.

1814.—Brooklyn ferry-boats adopted steam.

Specie payments were suspended for nearly three years.

1815.—New York received with enthusiasm, the news of a treaty of peace between the United States and Great Britain.

Thirteen Insurance Companies were located in Wall Street.

1816.—The Common Council of New York prohibited chimney-sweepers from crying their trade in the streets.

Enormous importations of merchandise from Europe rendered this year a memorable one among commercial men.

1817.—The first regular packet-ships, called the Black Ball Line, sailed between New York and Liverpool.

An Asylum for the deaf and dumb was incorporated.

1818.—Shoe pegs were introduced.

1819.—The first ocean steamship, the "Savannah," crossed the Atlantic from New York to Liverpool.

The first Savings Bank was opened.

1820.—The population of New York was one hundred and twenty-three thousand, seven hundred and six.

New York and New Orleans were connected by a line of steamships.

The *New York Observer* was published.

Fire-proof safes, constructed of iron and wood, were imported from France.

Daily mails were established between New York, and Brooklyn and Jamaica, Long Island.

The Old Park Theatre was burned.

1821.—In January, the North River from Cortlandt Street to Jersey City, was crossed on the ice by loaded sleighs.

1822.—New York, with other counties, had a separate District Attorney.

A steamship line carried passengers and freight between New York and Norfolk.

1823.—The first steam-power printing press in the United States was put in operation. An abridgement of Murray's English Grammar was the first work done by this machine.

The New York Gas-Light Company was incorporated.

1824.—A House of Refuge for the reformation of juvenile delinquents was erected by private subscription. This was the beginning of a new system for the correction of the vices of the young.

General Lafayette was welcomed with great rejoicing as the guest of the city and nation.

1825.—October 26th, the sound of cannon, first heard at Buffalo, and then repeated from point to point, announced the completion of the Erie Canal, and the union of the Great Lakes with the Atlantic. The arrival in New York City of the first canal-boat was the occasion of a grand aquatic and civil pageant, in which the "commingling of the waters," was typically illustrated by Governor De Witt Clinton, the "Father of the Canal," who, amidst impressive ceremonies, poured from a keg the water of Lake Erie, into the ocean at the Narrows.

The first Sunday newspaper published in this city was issued under the name of the *Sunday Courier*. It was soon discontinued for want of patronage.

The first performance of Italian Opera was given at the Park Theatre.

Homœopathy was introduced by a physician from Denmark.

The tinder-box,, which had been the implement used for lighting fires, was superseded by a bottle filled with acid and cotton, and surmounted by phosphorized pine sticks.

The quintal of one hundred, instead of one hundred and twelve pounds, was adopted by the merchants as the new measure for purchase and sale.

Gas mains were laid in Broadway.

1827.—The *Journal of Commerce* and the *Morning Inquirer* were started. These two papers, in their efforts to rival each other, established swift schooners and pony-expresses for the purpose of obtaining the commercial news.

1828.—The Law Institute was organized.

Webster's Dictionary was published.

Varnish was first manufactured.

1829.—The American Institute was incorporated, and held its first fair.

Bricks were manufactured by machinery.

Galvanized iron was invented.

1830.—A railroad locomotive, the first one constructed in America, was built in New York for a railroad in South Carolina.

Omnibuses were introduced. The word "omnibus," painted in large letters on both sides of the vehicle, was generally supposed to be that of the owner.

The *Christian Intelligencer*, an organ of the Dutch Reformed Church, published its first number.

1831.—A street railroad was completed, and opened for travel, between the City Hall and 14th Street.

The first sporting paper, called *The Spirit of the Times*, was issued.

The New York and Harlem Railroad Company was incorporated.

1832.—Peter Cooper, the philanthropist, demonstrated to the stockholders of the Albany and Schenectady Railroad, that cars could be drawn around short curves.

Five thousand persons died from Asiatic cholera.

1833.—The *New York Sun*, a penny paper, was published.

1834.—A meeting of the American Anti-Slavery Society was broken up by a mob

In conformity with an amendment of the Constitution, a mayor of New York was elected, for the first time by the votes of the people.

1835.—The *New York Herald* was founded.

Pins were manufactured by machinery.

A disastrous conflagration, destroying property to the extent of twenty millions of dollars, was checked only by blowing up several houses.

1836.—Work on the aqueduct was begun.

The Common Council ordered pipes to be laid, preparatory to the introduction of water into the city.

Commercial distress and financial panic spread over the whole country, and swept numerous firms out of existence.

1840.—A manufactory of gold pens was established.

The *New York Tribune*, edited by Horace Greely, was published. The receipts of this paper for the first week, were ninety-two dollars; the expenses amounted to five hundred and twenty-five dollars.

1841.—The "Princeton," a ship-of-war, was constructed by John Ericsson. This was the first ship in which the propelling machinery was placed under water, and secured from shot.

1842.—Abolitionists declared a separate nomination, held a State Convention, and ran a candidate for the mayoralty of New York.

June 27th, water was received through the

aqueduct into the reservoir at 86th Street, July 4th, it was introduced into the distributing-reservoir on Murray Hill, while waving flags, clanging bells, floral canopies, and songs, proclaimed the great interest which this event awakened. The fountain in the park, opposite the Astor House, consisted of a central pipe with eighteen subordinate jets, in a basin one hundred feet broad. By shifting the plate of the conduit pipe, the water assumed such shapes as the " Maid of the Mist," the " Croton Plume," the " Vase," the " Dome," the " Bouquet," the " Sheaf of Wheat," and the " Weeping Willow."

A similar display in Union Square, then called Union Park, was a weeping willow of crystal drops illuminated with fireworks that kindled the cloud of mist until it resembled showers of many colored gems.

1843.—A submarine telegraph connected New York with Fire Island and Coney Island.

A patent for a sewing machine that made a lasting stitch, was granted to a resident of the city.

1844.—An enormous immigration poured in from Ireland and other European countries, in consequence of famine and political disturbances.

1845.—A disastrous fire occurred, which destroyed a large amount of property.

1846.—The first granite-block pavement was laid.

1847.—The first sucessful type-revolving press was made by a resident of the city.

The Board of Education took action in reference to the establishment of a Free Academy. This was the first institution, maintained at the public expense, by which the pupils of the New York schools could secure the advantages of those higher departments of learning, usually obtained at great expense in the colleges.

1848.—The first Electric Telegraph Service was inaugurated.

1849.—The "Astor Place Riot" occurred.

The New York Press Association was formed.

The phenomenon of spirit-rapping caused much excitement.

1850.—P. T. Barnum introduced Jenny Lind to an enraptured audience.

An Arctic expedition sailed from New York in search of Franklin.

The American Bible Union was organized.

1851.—Kossuth, the Hungarian patriot, visited the city and received an enthusiastic welcome.

The *New York Times* appeared.

1853.—An International World's Fair was held in the Crystal Palace.

The New York Clearing House was organized by fifty-two of the city banks

1854.—The Astor Library was opened to the public.

1855.—Castle Garden was utilized as a receiving-depot for emigrants.

The ground for Central Park was selected by commissioners appointed by the Supreme Court.

1857.—An unsuccessful attempt to lay the Atlantic Cable was made, the wire parting when but three hundred and thirty-four miles had been paid out.

1858.—The successful laying of the Atlantic Cable was announced, and celebrated by public demonstration.

Crystal Palace was burned.

The voice of Adelina Patti was heard for the first time in public. The cantatrice had not then attained her seventeenth year.

1860.—The secession of South Carolina caused much consternation in business circles.

The Prince of Wales and his suite were welcomed with elaborate ceremony.

The Japanese Embassy visited the city.

1861.—Central Park was opened to the public.

The banks, having loaned enormous sums of money to the Government, suspended specie payments, after the attack upon Fort Sumter.

1863.—A draft in progress in the Ninth District, caused a riot among foreign laborers, who attacked the recruiting office, destroyed the wheel, scattered the lists, and set the building on fire. As the militia had been sent to Philadelphia to resist a Confederate invasion, the police were unaided, and could not suppress the demonstration for several days. One hundred persons were killed, and a large amount of property was destroyed.

1865.—News of the surrender of General Lee and the Confederate Army caused great rejoicing. Banners streamed in the wind, the national colors were displayed in great profusion, sweet bells chimed the airs of peace, the sound of cannon rolled over the water of the rivers and the bay, and the atmosphere was filled with the general gladness and mirth of the people.

One week from the time when peace was restored to the country, the body of President Lincoln was laid in state in the City Hall, the "Saviour of his Country" having been shot by an assassin, while in his box at the theatre in Washington. The tri-colored decorations of the city were at once exchanged for the sombre hues of woe.

1867.—In January, five thousand persons crossed over a bridge of ice that had formed in the East River between New York and Brooklyn.

A short experimental section of the Ninth Avenue Elevated Railroad was opened for travel.

1869.—The American Museum of Natural History was incorporated.

The Telegraph Messenger Service was organized.

1870.—The Metropolitan Museum of Art received its charter.

1872.—A committee of seventy was appointed to investigate the extent of the depredations made by Tweed and his "Ring," and to bring those criminals to justice.

1873.—The business interests of the city were paralyzed by a panic of unusual severity.

Morrisania, West Farms and Kingsbridge, three villages that covered an area nearly doubling that of the city, were annexed.

The city charter was amended, and many important modifications were made on previous enactments.

1875.—Fourth Avenue was improved at a cost of six millions of dollars, an expense shared equally by the city and the New York Central Railroad Company.

1876.—The one hundredth anniversary of the signing of the Declaration of Independence, celebrated by a World's Fair at Philadelphia, brought many visitors to the city. Exhibitions of loaned paintings, held in the Academy of Design and the Metropolitan Museum of Art during the summer season, made the year a memorable one to the lovers of fine art.

Hell Gate channel was opened.

1878.—The streets were lighted by electric arc-lamps.

1879.—The Central-Station Telephone service was put in operation.

1880.—Four elevated railroad lines were completed, and in operation.

1881.—The city, with the nation, was called to mourn the death of President Garfield, who was assassinated in Washington by an insane person.

The current was first turned on for the Incandescent Lamp Service.

Four hundred and forty-four newspapers and periodicals were published.

1883.—East River Bridge was opened to the public.

The statue of Washington, now standing upon the steps of the Sub-Treasury Building in Wall Street, was presented to the United States Government by the New York Chamber of Commerce, on the occasion of the one hundredth anniversary of the British evacuation of New York.

1888.—The city was visited by a storm of wind and snow that for several days shut off almost all communication with the surrounding country, and resulted in much suffering and many deaths.

1889.—An elaborate pageant, commemorating the first inauguration of a President of the United States, arrayed New York in holiday attire, and provided for its citizens three days of patriotic display and memorable pleasure.

The programme included civil and religious ceremonies, a naval, a military, and a civil parade, and terminated with a great ball at the Metropolitan Opera House. It is estimated that three million strangers visited the city during the time of this celebration.

1890.—The population of the city, as reported in the United States census, has been as follows:

1790	33,131
1800	60,489
1810	96,373
1820	123,706
1830	197,112
1840	312,710
1850	515,547
1860	813,669
1870	942,292
1880	1,206,299
1890	1,515,301

An enumeration made by the police, under the unanimous resolution of the Common Council, showed the population of 1890 to have been 1,710,715.

The credit obtained by the city was illustrated by an achievement never before reached in the history of municipal finance, bonds bearing interest at two and one-half per cent. having been sold in the open market at a premium of one and one-eighth per cent.

A "strike" by the engineers of the New York Central Railroad closed transportation over that route for several days.

1891.—A Cable Railroad was laid from the Battery to Central Park.

GENERAL HISTORY OF THE SOCIAL DEVELOPMENT OF THE CITY OF NEW YORK.

THE appearance, customs, and manners, of the people who occupied Manhattan Island before the coming of the white settlers, were so distinct from those of other nations known to the civilized world, and their individual character had so little in common with the more restrained and law-abiding Europeans, that they were classed among those wild and lawless races who, it was supposed, had few of the affections and higher emotions of humanity. Later experience, however, has shown that under the advantages of education and moral culture, the American Indian is capable of high attainments in all that distinguishes the best traits of human character.

The huts or wigwams of these Aborigines were made of two rows of upright saplings, with the branches brought together at the top. Upon this frame-work a lathing of boughs was fastened, and the inside was nicely covered by strips of bark that afforded a good protection from wind and rain. The ground was the only flooring these habitations contained, and on this fires were kindled, the smoke escaping through an aperture in the roof. The width of the wigwams was always twenty feet, the length varied according to the number of persons that they were designed to accommodate. Sometimes twenty or thirty families occupied the same apartment, each retaining an allotted space. In time of war a fence or stockade, from ten to fifteen feet in height, protected the villages.

The Manhattan Indians are described as having been tall, small at the waist, with black or dark-brown eyes, snow-white teeth and cinnamon-colored skins. They were active and sprightly, though probably of less average strength than Europeans of the same size. While eating they sat upon the ground, taking the food with their fingers. In their dress they were fond of display, both sexes indulging in this taste to an extravagant degree. Some of the highly ornamented petticoats of the women were sold to the early settlers for eighty dollars. The men wore upon their shoulders a mantle of deer-skin, with the fur next to their bodies, the outside of the garment exhibiting a variety of painted designs. Sometimes these queer people decorated themselves with many colors and patterns. In "full paint" they were both grotesque and frightful. The procurement of food, which consisted of nuts, fruit, fish, and game, was the usual employment in time of peace. The bow and arrow were the implements used in hunting. It is said that the Indian boys attained great skill with these weapons, being able to hit a shilling at a distance of fifty feet. This singular expertness was a wonder to the white settlers, who sometimes excited emulation among them by tossing up a purse of money to be claimed by whoever could hit it in the air.

After death the Indians were placed sitting, in graves lined with boughs, and covered with stones and earth. By their side were deposited cooking utensils, money, and food, in order that the spirit might want for nothing on its journey to the "Happy Hunting Grounds."

The original name for the Island was Monaton, a word descriptive of the whirlpool at Hell Gate,— the most striking geographical feature of the region,—and the appellation by which the earliest inhabitants designated themselves was "Mon-a-tuns," or "People of the Whirlpool." Manhattan is the Anglicized term.

FROM 1613 TO 1664.

Some of the early settlers adopted the bark cabins of the savages, while others dwelt temporarily in roofed cellars. After a saw-mill was built near a stream that emptied into the East River opposite Blackwell's Island, these pioneers constructed one-story log dwellings, the roofs of which were thatched with straw, and the chimneys made

DUTCH DWELLINGS IN NEW AMSTERDAM.

of wood. The windows admitted light through oiled paper.

As the little town of New Amsterdam increased in size, its habitations assumed a more substantial and comfortable aspect, tiles, shingles, and even brick, having been used for the most elaborate residences. The houses were built in the Low Dutch style, with the gable ends toward the street, the tops indented like stairs, the roofs surmounted by a weathercock, and the walls clamped with iron designed in the form of letters, (usually the initials of the proprietor's name), and in figures indicating the year when the building was erected. Every house was surrounded with a garden in which both flowers and vegetables were cultivated. Cows and swine were abundant, but horses were very rare. Inside, the floors were strewn with clean sand. Cupboards and chests that held the pewter plate, or household linen, were the main ornaments of the best room, and as wealth increased, some of these displayed china tea-sets, and pieces of solid silver.

According to Lossing: "Clocks and watches were almost unknown, and time was measured by sun-dials and hour-glasses. The habits of the people were so regular that they did not need clocks and watches. At nine o'clock they all said their prayers and went to bed. They arose at cock-crowing, and breakfasted before sunrise. Dinner-parties were unknown, but tea-parties were frequent. These ended, the participants went home in time to attend to the milking of the cows. In every house were spinning-wheels, and it was the pride of every family to have an ample supply of home-made linen and woollen cloth. The women spun and wove, and were steadily employed. Nobody was idle. Nobody was anxious to get rich, while all practised thrift and frugality. Books were rare luxuries, and in most houses the bible and prayer-book constituted the stock of literature. The weekly discourses of the clergyman satisfied their intellectual wants, while their own hands, industriously employed, furnished all their physical necessities. Knitting and spinning held the place of whist and music in these "degenerate days," and utility was as plainly stamped upon all their labors and pleasures as is the maker's name on our silver spoons. These were the "good old days" of simplicity, comparative innocence, and positive ignorance, when the "commonalty" no more suspected the earth of the caper of turning over like a ball of yarn every day than Stuyvesant did the Puritans of candor and honesty."

Most of the streets were paved to the width of ten feet from the fronts of the houses, the middle space containing public wells, and being left without pavement, for the more easy absorption of water. Brick pathways, called "strookes," were laid in place of sidewalks. Public markets were quite numerous, the supply having been received from the fertile section of country on the northern portion of the Island, where the farmers located a village called New Harlem. The road to this settlement was little more than an Indian trail leading through the woods, and becoming impassable in many seasons.

As to the character of these founders of the city of New York, they were deliberate, but determined. Much time was spent in examining every project before it was ventured upon, but when once undertaken it was carried out with a spirit of force and persistence to which later generations are deeply indebted.

With regard to the people of Holland, Mrs. Martha Lamb, in her "History of New York," asserts: "In no country were the domestic and social ties of life discharged with greater precision. It matters not that chroniclers have made the Dutch subjects of unmerited depreciation. It has been stated that they were characterized only by slowness; and that the land was barren of invention, progress or ideas. The seeds of error and prejudice thus sown bear little fruit after the reading of a few chapters of genuine contemporary personal description. As a rule the Hollanders were not inclined to take the initiative in trade or politics, and were distinguished for solidity rather than brilliancy; but it is absurd to say they were unequal to the origination of any new thing. We find among them many of the most illustrious men of modern Europe,—politicians, warriors, scholars, artists, and divines. Wealth was widely diffused; learning was held in high respect; and eloquence, courage and public spirit were characteristic of the race. For nearly a century after the Dutch Republic took its place among independent nations, it swayed the balance of European politics; and the acumen and culture of the leading statesmen elicited universal deference and admiration. For an index to the private life of the upper classes, we need to take a peep into the richly furnished apartments of their stately mansions, or walk through their summer-houses and choice conservatories and famous picture galleries. As for the peasantry, they were neat to a fault and industrious, as well as frugal."

It will not be amiss in this connection to quote from the historian Broadhead, who says about the women of Holland; " The purity of morals and decorum of manners for which the Dutch have ever been conspicuous, may be most justly ascribed to the happy influence of their women, who mingled in all the active affairs of life, and were consulted with deferential respect. They loved their homes and their firesides, but they loved their country more. Through all their toils and struggles, the calm fortitude of the men of Holland was nobly encouraged and sustained by the earnest and undaunted spirit of their mothers and wives. And the empire which the female sex obtained was no greater than that which their beauty, good sense, virtue, and devotion entitled them to hold."

FROM 1664 TO 1776.

The advent of the British brought about many beneficial changes in the social life of the Island. Not only were English habits incorporated into the less ambitious character of the Dutch inhabitants, but the settlement of many Huguenot families of distinction aided materially to produce an atmosphere of culture. Irrepressible social, political, and religious, forces were sweeping over the great nations of Europe and imbuing the immigrants who sought our shores, with a spirit which was to work out undreamed of results. Founded upon Dutch stubbornness, integrity, and practicality,—supplemented by English inflexibility, sagacity, and commercial prosperity, and adorned by French refinement and vivacity,—it is no wonder that later generations arose to prominence, acquired the independence of character that could successfully resist oppression, and developed the ability to aid in founding and maintaining a new and marvellously prosperous nation.

As early as 1668 a social club composed of the best Dutch, English, and French families, was established. Meetings were held twice every week at the different houses, the members coming together about six, and separating at nine o'clock in the evening. The English governors and their suites held elaborate court, observing on all occasions the strictest etiquette sanctioned by foreign custom. Chroniclers love to dwell on this period of colonial history, in which the grand dames and lordly gentlemen appear in bold relief, not only because they were so few, but also for the reason that they were of the brightest and best that the earth afforded.

Quite a number of these personages brought with them considerable wealth, so that their residences became somewhat palatial, and adorned with furniture and works of art imported from Europe. Silver and gold plate, elaborate table service, and profuse entertainment, made New York hospitality famous even in European circles. Many families retired to country homes, where they lived in quiet but elegant simplicity, cultivating their farms, and entertaining with delightful courtesy their visitors from the city or from European countries.

The manners and customs of the less favored class of citizens were marked by industry, sobriety, and economy. At their festivals children and negroes were permitted the enjoyment of unrestrained mirth. Sunday gowns were removed as soon as their owners returned from church, and consequently were kept in a state of preservation which made it possible to hand them down as heirlooms. Cocked hats were treated with the same deferential regard. To illustrate the extreme simplicity of habit which prevailed among the people of this generation, it is only necessary to add that the Rev. Dr. Laidlie preached "right lustily against the luxurious abominations of suppers of chocolate and bread that kept the families till nine o'clock at night." This same preacher was the first divine who introduced the "outlandish practice of delivering his sermon in English."

The laws at this period were few, but rigorously enforced. A ride on a great wooden horse was

MANHATTAN.

This is a true picture of y^e new Ingen

                             C. Kortlandt
                                T. Ingen

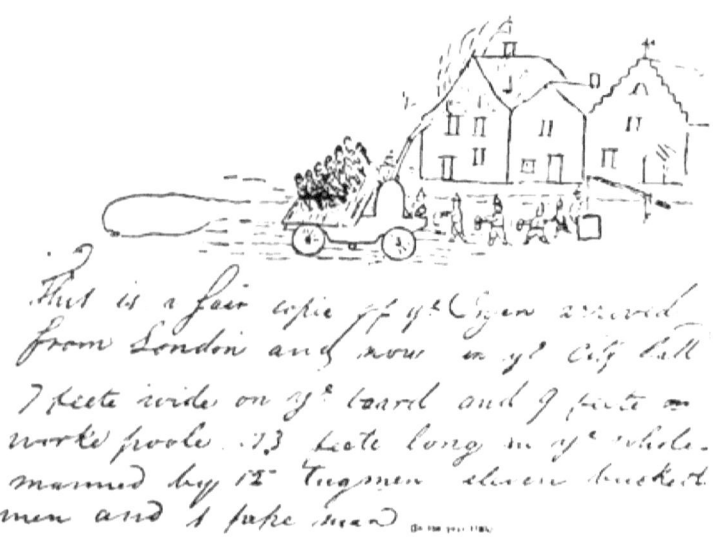

This is a fair copie of y^e Ingen arrived from London and now in y^e City Hall 7 feete wide on y^e board and 9 feete on worke poole 13 feete long in y^e whole, manned by 12 Tugmen eleven bucket men and 1 pipe man

the most common punishment. Every man pleaded his own cause, or what was more common, said little and let it take its own course. The only long speech on record is that of a certain pettifogger, who in pleading for the right of geese to swim in the pond at the head of "Nieuw" Street, did "incontinently cause his client to be non-suited, by tiring his worship's patience to such a degree that he fell into a deep sleep and slept out the remainder of the term."

The customs and dress of the period immediately preceding the Revolution are best described by Mrs. Lamb, as follows: "Show and glitter marked the distinctions in society. Dress was one of the signs and symbols of a gentleman; classical lore and ruffled shirts were inseparable. It was the habit of the community to take off its hat to the gentry; and there was no mistaking them wherever they moved. Servants were always in livery, which in many instances was gorgeous in the extreme. Gentlemen appeared in the streets in velvet or satin coats, with white embroidered vests of rare beauty, small clothes and gorgeously resplendent buckles, their heads crowned with powdered wigs and cocked hats. A lady's toilet was equally astounding; the court hoop was in vogue, brocaded silks of brilliant colors, and a mountain of powdered hair surmounted with flowers or feathers. Although it is a fact worthy of remembrance that servants were servants in those days, and never assumed to copy or excel their mistresses in the style and costliness of their attire, the democratic hammer already suspended over the doomed city was to subdue the taste and change the whole aspect of the empire of fashion."

At the time of the war, "Washington's guard

wore blue coats faced with buff, red waistcoats, buckskin breeches, black felt hats bound with white tape, and bayonet and body belts of white. Hunting shirts—"the martial aversion of the redcoat"—with breeches of same, with cloth gaiter-fashion about the legs, were seen on every side, and being convenient garments for a campaigning country, were soon adopted by the British themselves. This was the origin of the modern trouser or pantaloon."

FROM 1783 TO THE PRESENT TIME.

After the evacuation of the British and the restoration of peace, the city occupied itself incessantly with the work of reconstruction. During the residence of the chief executive the same punctilious ceremony was observed that had marked the English occupancy. The staid Knickerbocker element also dominated sufficiently to hold in check many tendencies that grew with marvellous rapidity under the stimulus of newly acquired independence, and the friction of a cosmopolitan life.

There is little to relate of special mannerism from this time. The increase of population differentiated social life into circles, each of which preserved its special code, and this tendency has of course increased until the present time, when innumerable cliques separate society, or draw together those whose temperaments and occupations make them congenial to each other.

The commercial development of the metropolis during the present century is a subject upon which volumes might be written and the half not told; indeed, the history of this period contains little else, although educational institutions have kept pace with the phenomenal prosperity. Efforts to encourage scholarship have been many and well founded, and the patronage of art has been liberal, advances steadily, and tends permanently to elevate the public taste.

At the present time the city extends from the Battery to Yonkers, including an area of forty and one-third square miles within its corporate limits. This territory is divided into twenty-four wards, designated by numbers, and into nearly one hundred and fifty thousand lots. Thirty-nine public parks, exclusive of triangles and small spaces, occupy a combined area of four thousand, eight hundred and forty-one acres. Pelham Bay Park, a tract consisting of seventeen hundred acres of forest land, with nine miles of water front along the Sound, has but recently been acquired. The annual appropriation for the maintenance of these pleasure resorts exceeds one million dollars.

The main configuration of the leading thoroughfares from the ancient "Copsie" or Battery, northward to the park, and thence to Harlem, Bloomingdale, and onward, were the old post-roads over which travellers passed to Boston and Albany. These highways followed the primary Indian trails.

There are now in New York from fifty to sixty thousand business firms, nearly one hundred and twenty thousand buildings, forty-five first-class theatres, two hundred first-class hotels, three thousand apartment-houses, five thousand clubs, societies, etc., six hundred and forty-nine newspapers and periodicals, fifty-three public libraries, very nearly five hundred churches, three hundred and thirty-seven thousand, three hundred and sixteen tenement houses, and forty-three cemeteries.

As to the future of the city, who can estimate its gigantic possibilities? Already the population is so dense as to render the present facilities for transportation quite inadequate. At the present moment there are no less than ten projects under discussion, or in process of construction, for conveying passengers and freight to and from New York and Long Island, or Jersey City, by way of vast bridges over the intervening rivers, or by tunnels under them. Rapid transit in every case is to be a certain result if these efforts achieve successful issues, and the constant pressure of necessity will doubtless insure a speedy completion for some of them.

The creation of a so-called "Greater New York," by the consolidation into one municipality of New York, Brooklyn, Staten Island, a portion of Westchester County, and a large area on Long Island, is a plan which awakens general interest at the present moment. The area of the consolidation would be three hundred and eighteen square miles, —a territory roughly estimated to include a radius of sixteen miles from the City Hall, (with the exception of that portion which lies within the State of New Jersey). The community would then be composed of three millions of people controlled by a central government.

Great educational institutions also contemplate the combination of their forces. New and beautiful edifices that will accommodate the growing demand for scholastic opportunities, soon are to be erected upon favorable sites uptown. Public buildings are to be discarded for more commodious quarters, and as many of these are required to be located in central parts of the city, familiar landmarks again must disappear, and nothing be left to the decay of age.

The march of progress brings with it as well, active individuals eager to promote the public good. Reformatory measures are inaugurated,— men and women both investigating deeply in order to better understand the methods whereby their wise ends may be gained,—and best of all, the voice of an ever-increasing multitude making itself heard in affairs, assures us that a diffused and widespread interest exists. This it is which surely promises in the time to come, a city the like of which has never yet been seen.

www.ingramcontent.com/pod-product-compliance
Lightning Source LLC
Chambersburg PA
CBHW020800230426
43666CB00007B/786